King Henry the 5th

By William Shakespeare

Edited by Julien Coallier

Copyright Julien Coallier 2012

All Rights Reserved.

Characters

Alice, a lady attending on Princess Katherine

All

Archbishop of Canterbury

Bardolph

Bates, soldier in King Henry's army

Bishop of Ely

Boy

Chorus

Constable of France

Court, soldier in King Henry's army

Duke of Bedford, brother to Henry IV, uncle to Henry V

Duke of Bourbon

Duke of Burgundy

Duke of Exeter, uncle to Henry IV, great-uncle to Henry V

Duke of Gloucester, brother to the King

Duke of Orleans

Duke of York, cousin to the king

Earl of Cambridge

Earl of Salisbury

Earl of Warwick

Earl of Westmoreland

Falstaff, Sir John Falstaff

First Ambassador

Fluellen

French Soldier

Governor of Harfleur

Gower

Grandpre, French lord

Henry V, Prince, King of England

Herald

Hostess Quickly, hostess of a tavern in Eastcheap

Jamy

Katharine, daughter to Charles and Isabel

King of France, Charles VI

Lewis the Dauphin

Lord Scroop

Macmorris

Messenger

Montjoy, a French herald

Nym, sharper attending on Falstaff

Pistol

Queen Isabel

Rambures, French lord

Sir Thomas Erpingham

Sir Thomas Grey

Williams, soldier in King Henry's army

Scenes

Intro – Page 9

Act I -

Scene 1. London. An ante-chamber in the KING'S palace.
Scene 2. The same. The Presence chamber.

Act II

Intro – Page 31
Scene 1. London. A street.
Scene 2. Southampton. A council-chamber.
Scene 3. London. Before a tavern.
Scene 4. France. The KING'S palace.

Act III

Intro – Page 65
Scene 1. France. Before Harfleur.
Scene 2. The same.
Scene 3. The same. Before the gates.
Scene 4. The FRENCH KING's palace.
Scene 5. The same.
Scene 6. The English camp in Picardy.
Scene 7. The French camp, near Agincourt:

Act IV

Intro – Page 111
Scene 1. The English camp at Agincourt.
Scene 2. The French camp.
Scene 3. The English camp.
Scene 4. The field of battle.
Scene 5. Another part of the field.
Scene 6. Another part of the field.
Scene 7. Another part of the field.
Scene 8. Before KING HENRY'S pavilion.

Act V

Intro – Page 175
Scene 1. France. The English camp.
Scene 2. France. A royal palace.

Finally – Page 205

Act 1 Intro

(Chorus enters)

Chorus

Oh for a Muse of fire that would ascend the brightest heaven of invention

A kingdom for a stage, princes to act and monarchs to behold the swelling scene!

Then should the warlike Harry, like himself, Assume the port of Mars

And at his heels, leashed in like hounds, should famine, sword, and fire crouch for employment

But pardon, and gentles all, the flat unraised spirits that have dared on this unworthy scaffold to bring forth so great an object, can this cockpit hold the vasty fields of France?

Or may we cram within this wooden oh the very helmets that did affright the air at Agincourt?

Oh, pardon! Since a crooked figure may attest in little place a million

And let us, ciphers to this great account, on your imaginary forces work.

Suppose within the girdle of these walls are now confined two mighty monarchies, whose high upreared and abutting fronts the perilous narrow ocean parts asunder, piece out our imperfections with your thoughts

Into a thousand parts divide on man, and make imaginary puissance

Think when we talk of horses, that you see them printing their proud hoofs in the receiving earth

For it is your thoughts that now must deck our kings, carry them here and there; jumping over times, turning the accomplishment of many years into an hour-glass, for the which supply, admit me Chorus to this history; who prologue-like your humble patience pray, gently to hear, kindly to judge, our play.

(Exit)

Act 1 Scene 1

London. An ante-chamber in the King's palace.

(The Archbishop of Canterbury, and the Bishop of Ely enter)

Canterbury

My lord, I'll tell you

That self bill is urged, which in the eleventh year of the last king's reign was like, and had indeed against us passed, but that the scambling and unquiet time did push it out of farther question.

Ely

But how, my lord, shall we resist it now?

Canterbury

It must be thought on.

If it pass against us we lose the better half of our possession for all the temporal lands which men devoutby testament have given to the church would they strip from us

Being valued thus as much as would maintain to the king's honour

Full fifteen earls and fifteen hundred knights, six thousand and two hundred good esquires and to relief of lazars and weak age, of indigent faint souls past corporal toil.

A hundred almshouses right well supplied and to the coffers of the king beside a thousand pounds by the year thus runs the bill.

Ely

This would drink deep.

Canterbury

It would drink the cup and all.

Ely

But what prevention?

Canterbury

The king is full of grace and fair regard.

Ely

And a true lover of the holy church.

Canterbury

The courses of his youth promised it not.

The breath no sooner left his father's body, but that his wildness, mortified in him seemed to die too

Yea, at that very moment consideration like an angel, came and whipped the offending Adam out of him, leaving his body as a paradise to envelop and contain celestial spirits.

Never was such a sudden scholar made

Never came reformation in a flood with such a heady currance, scouring faults nor never Hydra-headed willfulness, so soon did lose his seat and all at once as in this king.

Ely

We are blessed in the change.

Canterbury

Hear him but reason in divinity, and all-admiring with an inward wis you would desire the king were made a prelate, hear him debate of commonwealth affairs you would say it hath been all in all his study, list his discourse of war, and you shall hear a fearful battle rendered you in music

Turn him to any cause of policy, the Gordian knot of it he will unloose familiar as his garter

That, when he speaks the air, a chartered libertine, is still,

and the mute wonder lurketh in men's ears to steal his sweet and honeyed sentences

So that the art and practic part of life must be the mistress to this theoric, which is a wonder how his grace should glean it.

Since his addiction was to courses vain his companies unlettered, rude and shallow, his hours filled up with riots, banquets, sports, and never noted in him any study,

Any retirement, any sequestration from open haunts and popularity.

Ely

The strawberry grows underneath the nettle and wholesome berries thrive and ripen best neighbour'd by fruit of baser quality, and so the prince obscured his contemplation under the veil of wildness

Which, no doubt, grew like the summer grass, fastest by night unseen, yet crescive in his faculty.

Canterbury

It must be so

For miracles are ceased

And therefore we must needs admit the means of how things are perfected

Ely

But, my good lord, how now for mitigation of this bill urged by the commons?

Doth his majesty incline to it, or no?

Canterbury

He seems indifferent, or rather swaying more upon our part than cherishing the exhibiters against us

For I have made an offer to his majesty, upon our spiritual convocation and in regard of causes now in hand, which I have opened to his grace at large as touching France to give a greater sum than ever at one time the clergy, yet did to his predecessors part withal.

Ely

How did this offer seem received, my lord?

Canterbury

With good acceptance of his majesty

Save that there was not time enough to hear as I perceived his grace would fain have done the severals and unhidden passages of his true titles to some certain dukedoms

And generally to the crown and seat of France derived from Edward, his great-grandfather

Ely

What was the impediment that broke this off?

Canterbury

The French ambassador upon that instant craved audience

And the hour, I think, is come to give him hearing

Is it four o'clock?

Ely

It is.

Canterbury

Then go we in to know his embassy

Which I could with a ready guess declare before the Frenchman speak a word of it.

Ely

I'll wait upon you, and I long to hear it.

(Exit)

Act 1 Scene 2

The Presence chamber.

(King Henry 5, Gloucester, Bedford, Exeter, Warwick, Westmoreland, and Attendants enter)

King Henry 5

Where is my gracious Lord of Canterbury?

Exeter

Not here in presence.

King Henry 5

Send for him, good uncle.

Westmoreland

Shall we call in the ambassador, my liege?

King Henry 5

Not yet my cousin, we would be resolved before we hear him, of some things of weight that task our thoughts concerning us and France.

(The Archbishop of Canterbury, and the Bishop of Ely enter)

Canterbury

God and his angels guard your sacred throne and make you long become it!

King Henry 5

Sure, we thank you.

My learned lord, we pray you to proceed and justly and religiously unfold why the law Salique that they have in France or should, or should not, bar us in our claim

And God forbid, my dear and faithful lord, that you should fashion, wrest, or bow your reading or nicely charge your understanding soul with opening titles miscreate, whose right suits not in native colours with the truth

For God doth know how many now in health shall drop their blood in approbation of what your reverence shall incite us to.

Therefore take heed how you impawn our person, how you awake our sleeping sword of war, we charge you, in the name of God, take heed

For never two such kingdoms did contend without much fall of blood

Whose guiltless drops are every one a woe, a sore complaint against him whose wrong gives edge unto the swords that make such waste in brief mortality.

Under this conjuration, speak, my lord

For we will hear, note and believe in heart that what you speak is in your conscience washed as pure as sin with baptism.

Canterbury

Then hear me gracious sovereign, and you peers that owe yourselves your lives and services to this imperial throne.

There is no bar to make against your highness' claim to France but this, which they produce from Pharamond, 'No woman shall succeed in Salique land'

Which Salique land the French unjustly gloze to be the realm of France, and Pharamond the founder of this law and female bar

Yet their own authors faithfully affirm that the land Salique is in Germany, between the floods of Sala and of Elbe

Where Charles the Great, having subdued the Saxons,

there left behind and settled certain French

Who, holding in disdain the German women for some dishonest manners of their life, established then this law

To wit, no female should be inheritrix in Salique land, which Salique as I said, 'twixt Elbe and Sala is at this day in Germany called Meisen.

Then doth it well appear that Salique lawwWas not devised for the realm of France, nor did the French possess the Salique land until four hundred one and twenty years after defunction of King Pharamond,

Idly supposed the founder of this law

Who died within the year of our redemption four hundred twenty-six

And Charles the Great subdued the Saxons, and did seat the French beyond the river Sala in the year eight hundred five.

Besides, their writers say King Pepin, which deposed Childeric, did as heir general being descended

of Blithild, which was daughter to King Clothair,

making claim and title to the crown of France.

Hugh Capet also, who usurped the crown of Charles the duke of Lorraine, sole heir male of toe true line and stock of Charles the Great, to find his title with some shows of truth,

In through, in pure truth, it was corrupt and naught, conveyd himself as heir to the Lady Lingare, Daughter to Charlemain, who was the son to Lewis the emperor, and Lewis the son of Charles the Great.

Also King Lewis the Tenth, who was sole heir to the usurper Capet could not keep quiet in his conscience, wearing the crown of France till satisfied that fair Queen Isabel, his grandmother, was lineal of the Lady Ermengare, Daughter to Charles the foresaid duke of Lorraine

By the which marriage the line of Charles the Great was re-united to the crown of France.

So that, as clear as is the summer's sun…

King Pepin's title and Hugh Capet's claim, King Lewis his satisfaction, all appear to hold in right and title of the female, so do the kings of France unto this day

How-be-it they would hold up this Salique law to bar your highness claiming from the female, and rather choose to hide them in a net than amply to imbar their crooked titles, usurp'd from you and your progenitors.

King Henry 5

May I with right and conscience make this claim?

Canterbury

The sin upon my head, dread sovereign!

For in the book of Numbers is it writ, when the man dies let the inheritance descend unto the daughter.

Gracious lord, stand for your own

Unwind your bloody flag

Look back into your mighty ancestors, go my dread lord, to your great-grandsire's tomb from whom you claim

Invoke his warlike spirit and your great-uncle's, Edward the Black Prince, who on the French ground played a tragedy, making defeat on the full power of France; whiles his most mighty father on a hill stood smiling to behold his lion's whelp forage in blood of French nobility.

Oh noble English.

That could entertain with half their forces the full Pride of France and let another half stand laughing by, all out of work and cold for action!

Ely

Awake remembrance of these valiant dead and with your puissant arm renew their feats, you are their heir;

You sit upon their throne

The blood and courage that renowned them runs in your veins

And my thrice-puissant liege is in the very may-morn of his youth, ripe for exploits and mighty enterprises.

Exeter

Your brother kings and monarchs of the earth do all expect that you should rouse yourself, as did the former lions of your blood.

Westmoreland

They know your grace hath cause and means and might

So hath your highness

Never king of England had nobles richer and more loyal subjects, whose hearts have left their bodies here in England and lie pavilioned in the fields of France.

Canterbury

Oh, let their bodies follow, my dear liege with blood and sword and fire to win your right

In aid whereof we of the spiritualty will raise your highness such a mighty sum as never did the clergy at one time bring in to any of your ancestors.

King Henry 5

We must not only arm to invade the French, but lay down our proportions to defend against the Scot, who will make road upon us with all advantages.

Canterbury

They of those marches, gracious sovereign, shall be a wall sufficient to defend our inland from the pilfering borderers.

King Henry 5

We do not mean the coursing snatchers only, but fear the main intendment of the Scot who hath been still a giddy neighbour to us

For you shall read that my great-grandfather bever went with his forces into France but that the Scot on his unfurnished kingdom came pouring, like the tide into a breach, with ample and brim fulness of his force, galling the gleaned land with hot assays, girding with grievous siege castles and towns

That England, being empty of defence, hath shook and trembled at the ill neighbourhood

Canterbury

She hath been then more feared than harmed, my liege

For hear her but exampled by herself, when all her chivalry hath been in France and she a mourning widow of her nobles, she hath herself not only well defended but taken and impounded as a stray the King of Scots

Whom she did send to France, to fill King Edward's fame with prisoner kings and make her chronicle as rich with praise as is the ooze and bottom of the sea with sunken wreck and sunless treasuries

Westmoreland

But there's a saying very old and true, If that you will France win then with Scotland first begin, for once the eagle England being in prey, to her unguarded nest the weasel Scot comes sneaking and so sucks her princely eggs, playing the mouse in absence of the cat to tear and havoc more than she can eat.

Exeter

It follows then the cat must stay at home, yet that is but a crushed necessity since we have locks to safeguard necessaries, and pretty traps to catch the petty thieves.

While that the armed hand doth fight abroad, the advised head defends itself at home

For government, though high and low and lower, put into parts, doth keep in one consent, congreeing in a full and natural close like music.

Canterbury

Therefore doth heaven divide the state of man in divers functions, setting endeavour in continual motion

To which is fixed, as an aim or butt, obedience, for so work the honey-bees, creatures that by a rule in nature teach the act of order to a peopled kingdom.

They have a king and officers of sorts

Where some like magistrates correct at home, others like merchants venture trade abroad, others like soldiers armed in their stings make boot upon the summer's velvet buds, which pillage they with merry march bring home to the tent-royal of their emperor

Who, busied in his majesty, surveys the singing masons building roofs of gold, the civil citizens kneading up the honey, the poor mechanic porters crowding in their heavy burdens at his narrow gate, the sad-eyed justice with his surly hum delivering over to executors pale, the lazy yawning drone.

I thus infer, that many things, having full reference to one consent, may work contrariously

As many arrows loosed several ways come to one mark

As many ways meet in one town

As many fresh streams meet in one salt sea

As many lines close in the dial's centre

So may a thousand actions once afoot end in one purpose, and be all well borne without defeat.

Therefore to France, my liege

Divide your happy England into four

Whereof take you one quarter into France, and you withal shall make all Gallia shake.

If we, with thrice such powers left at home cannot defend our own doors from the dog, let us be worried and our nation lose the name of hardiness and policy.

King Henry 5

Call in the messengers sent from the Dauphin.

(Some Attendants exit)

Now are we well resolved

And by God's help and yours, the noble sinews of our power, France being ours, we'll bend it to our awe or break it all to pieces

Or there we'll sit, ruling in large and ample empery over France and all her almost kingly dukedoms, or lay these bones in an unworthy urn, tombless, with no remembrance over them

Either our history shall with full mouth speak freely of our acts, or else our grave, like Turkis mute, shall have a tongueless mouth not worshipped with a waxen epitaph.

(Ambassadors of France enter)

Now are we well prepared to know the pleasure of our fair cousin Dauphin

For we hear your greeting is from him, not from the king.

First Ambassador

May it please your majesty to give us leave, freely to render what we have in charge

Or shall we sparingly show you far off the Dauphin's meaning and our embassy?

King Henry 5

We are no tyrant, but a Christian king

Unto whose grace our passion is as subject zs are our wretches fettered in our prisons, therefore with frank and with uncurbed plainness tell us the Dauphin's mind.

First Ambassador

Thus, then, in few.

Your highness, lately sending into France did claim some certain dukedoms, in the right of your great predecessor, King Edward the Third.

In answer of which claim, the prince our master says that you savour too much of your youth, and bids you be advised there's nought in France that can be with a nimble galliard won

You cannot revel into dukedoms there.

He therefore sends you, meeter for your spirit, this turn of treasure

And, in lieu of this, desires you let the dukedoms that you claim hear no more of you.

This the Dauphin speaks.

King Henry 5

What treasure, uncle?

Exeter

Tennis-balls, my liege.

King Henry 5

We are glad the Dauphin is so pleasant with us

His present and your pains we thank you for, when we have marched our rackets to these balls, we will in France, by God's grace, play a set and shall strike his father's crown into the hazard.

Tell him he hath made a match with such a wrangler that all the courts of France will be disturbed with chances.

And we understand him well how he comes over us with our wilder days, not measuring what use we made of them.

We never valued this poor seat of England

And therefore, living hence, did give ourself to barbarous licence; as it is ever common that men are merriest when they are from home.

But tell the Dauphin I will keep my state, be like a king and show my sail of greatness when I do rouse me in my throne of France

For that I have laid by my majesty and plodded like a man for working-days, but I will rise there with so full a glory that I will dazzle all the eyes of France; yea strike the Dauphin blind to look on us.

And tell the pleasant prince this mock of his hath turned his balls to gun-stones

And his soul shall stand sore charged for the wasteful vengeance that shall fly with them, for many a thousand widows shall this his mock mock out of their dear husbands

Mock mothers from their sons, mock castles down

And some are yet ungotten and unborn that shall have cause to curse the Dauphin's scorn.

But this lies all within the will of God, to whom I do appeal

And in whose name tell you the Dauphin I am coming on, to venge me as I may and to put forth my rightful hand in a well-hallowed cause.

So get you hence in peace

And tell the Dauphin his jest will savour but of shallow wit, when thousands weep more than did laugh at it.

Convey them with safe conduct.

Fare you well.

(Ambassadors exit)

Exeter

This was a merry message.

King Henry 5

We hope to make the sender blush at it.

Therefore, my lords, omit no happy hour that may give furtherance to our expedition

For we have now no thought in us but France, save those to God that run before our business

Therefore let our proportions for these wars be soon collected and all things thought upon that may with reasonable swiftness add more feathers to our wings

For God before, we'll chide this Dauphin at his father's door.

Therefore let every man now task his thought, that this fair action may on foot be brought.

(Exit, Flourish)

Act 2 Intro

(Chorus enters)

Chorus

Now all the youth of England are on fire, and silken dalliance in the wardrobe lies

Now thrive the armourers, and honour's thought reigns solely in the breast of every man

They sell the pasture now to buy the horse, following the mirror of all Christian kings

With winged heels, as Englis Mercuries. for now sits Expectation in the air and hides a sword from hilts unto the point with crowns imperial, crowns and coronets, promised to Harry and his followers.

The French, advised by good intelligence of this most dreadful preparation, shake in their fear and with pale policy, seeks to divert the Englis purposes.

Oh England! model to thy inward greatness, like little body with a mighty heart, what mightst thou do, that honour would thee do, were all thy children kind and natural!

But see thy fault! France hath in thee found out a nest of hollow bosoms, which he fills with treacherous crowns

And three corrupted men, one Richard Earl of Cambridge, and the second, Henry Lord Scroop of Masham, and the third, Sir Thomas Grey, knight, of Northumberland…

Have for the gilt of France Oh guilt indeed!

Confirmed conspiracy with fearful France

And by their hands this grace of kings must die, if hell and treason hold their promises, here he take ship for France, and in Southampton.

Linger your patience on

And we'll digest the abuse of distance

Force a play

The sum is paid

The traitors are agreed

The king is set from London

And the scene is now transported, gentles, to Southampton

There is the playhouse now, there must you sit

And thence to France shall we convey you safe and bring you back, charming the narrow seas to give you gentle pass

For if we may, we'll not offend one stomach with our play

But till the king come forth, and not till then unto Southampton do we shift our scene. **(Exit)**

Act 2 Scene 1

London. A street.

(Corporal NYM and Lieutenant Bardolph enter)

Bardolph

Well met, Corporal Nym.

NYM

Good morrow, Lieutenant Bardolph.

Bardolph

What, are Ancient Pistol and you friends yet?

NYM

For my part I care not, I say little but when time shall serve, there shall be smiles.

But that shall be as it may.

I dare not fight, but I will wink and hold out mine iron, it is a simple one but what though? It will toast cheese, and it will endure cold as another man's sword will, and there's an end.

Bardolph

I will bestow a breakfast to make you friends and we'll be all three sworn brothers to France, let it be so, good Corporal Nym.

NYM

Faith, I will live so long as I may, that's the certain of it and when I cannot live any longer, I will do as I may, that is my rest, that is the rendezvous of it.

Bardolph

It is certain, corporal, that he is married to Nell Quickly: and certainly she did you wrong for you were troth-plight to her.

NYM

I cannot tell

Things must be as they may: men may sleep, and they may have their throats about them at that time and some say knives have edges. It must be as it may, though patience be a tired mare, yet she will plod.

There must be conclusions.

Well, I cannot tell.

(Pistol and Hostess enter)

Bardolph

Here comes Ancient Pistol and his wife: good corporal, be patient here.

How now, mine host Pistol!

Pistol

Base tike, call'st thou me host?

Now, by this hand, I swear, I scorn the term

Nor shall my Nell keep lodgers

Hostess

No, by my troth, not long

For we cannot lodge and board a dozen or fourteen gentlewomen that live honestly by the prick of their needles, but it will be thought we keep a bawdy house straight.

(NYM and Pistol draw)

Oh well a day, Lady, if he be not drawn now! We shall see wilful adultery and murder committed.

Bardolph

Good lieutenant! good corporal! offer nothing here.

NYM

Pish!

Pistol

Pis for thee, Iceland dog! thou prick-eared cur of Iceland!

Hostess

Good Corporal Nym, show thy valour, and put up your sword.

NYM

Will you shog off? I would have you solus.

Pistol

Soulless, arduous dog? Oh viper vile!

The soulless in thy most marvelous face

The soulless in thy teeth, and in thy throat, and in thy hateful lungs, yea in thy mouth lost which is worse, within thy nasty mouth!

I do retort the soulless in thy bowels

For I can take and Pistol's cock is up and flashing fire will follow.

NYM

I am not Barbason, you cannot conjure me.

I have a humour to knock you indifferently well.

If you grow foul with me, Pistol, I will scour you with my rapier, as I may in fair terms if you would walk off.

I would prick your guts a little, in good terms as I may and that's the humour of it.

Pistol

Oh braggart vile and damned furious wight!

The grave doth gape, and doting death is near therefore exhale

Bardolph

Hear me, hear me what I say, he that strikes the first stroke, I'll run him up to the hilts as I am a soldier.

(Draws)

Pistol

An oath of mickle might and fury shall abate. Give me thy fist, thy fore-foot to me give, thy spirits are most tall.

NYM

I will cut thy throat, one time or other in fair terms, that is the humour of it.

Pistol

Do or die

That is the word.

I thee defy again.

Oh hound of Crete, think'st thou my spouse to get?

No to the spital go, and from the powdering tub of infamy fetch forth the lazar kite of Cressid's kind, doll Tearsheet she by name, and her espouse I have, and I will hold, the quondam quickly for the only she and growth, there's enough.

Go to.

(The Boy enters)

Boy

Mine host Pistol, you must come to my master, and you hostess, he is very sick and would to bed.

Good Bardolph, put thy face between his sheets, and do the office of a warming-pan.

Have faith, he's very ill.

Bardolph

Away, you rogue!

Hostess

By my troth, he'll yield the crow a pudding one of these days.

The king has killed his heart.

Good husband, come home presently.

(Hostess and Boy exit)

Bardolph

Come, shall I make you two friends?

We must to France together, why the devil should we keep knives to cut one another's throats?

Pistol

Let floods overswell, and fiends for food howl on!

NYM

You'll pay me the eight shillings I won of you at betting?

Pistol

Base is the slave that pays.

NYM

That now I will have: that's the humour of it.

Pistol

As manhood shall compound: push home.

(They draw)

Bardolph

By this sword, he that makes the first thrust, I'll kill him by this sword, I will.

Pistol

Sword is an oath, and oaths must have their course.

Bardolph

Corporal Nym, an thou wilt be friends, be friends and thou wilt not, why then be enemies with me too.

I pray to thee, put up.

NYM

I shall have my eight shillings I won of you at betting?

Pistol

A noble shalt thou have, and present pay and liquor likewise will I give to thee and friendship shall combine, and brotherhood

I'll live by Nym, and Nym shall live by me, is not this just?

For I shall sutler be unto the camp, and profits will accrue.

Give me thy hand.

NYM

I shall have my noble?

Pistol

In cash most justly paid.

NYM

Well, then, that's the humour of it.

(Hostess re-enters)

Hostess

As ever you came of women, come in quickly to Sir John.

Ah, poor heart! he is so shaked of a burning quotidian tertian, that it is most lamentable to behold.

Sweet men, come to him.

NYM

The king hath run bad humours on the knight; that's the even of it.

Pistol

Nym, thou hast spoke the right, his heart is fracted and corroborate.

NYM

The king is a good king, but it must be as it may, he passes some humours and careers.

Pistol

Let us condole the knight; for, lambkins we will live.

Act 2 Scene 2

Southampton. A council-chamber.

(Exeter, Bedford, and Westmoreland enter)

Bedford

Before God, his grace is bold, to trust these traitors.

Exeter

They shall be apprehended by and by.

Westmoreland

How smooth and even they do bear themselves!

As if allegiance in their bosoms sat crowned with faith and constant loyalty.

Bedford

The king hath note of all that they intend, by interception, which they dream not of.

Exeter

Nay, but the man that was his bedfellow, whom he hath dulled and cloyed with gracious favours that he should for a foreign purse so sell his sovereign's life to death and treachery.

(Trumpets sound)

(King Henry 5, Scroop, Cambridge, Grey, and Attendants enter)

King Henry 5

Now sits the wind fair, and we will aboard.

My Lord of Cambridge, and my kind Lord of Masham, and you my gentle knight, give me your thoughts.

Think you not that the powers we bear with us will cut their passage through the force of France doing the execution and the act for which we have in head assembled them?

Scroop

No doubt, my liege, if each man do his best.

King Henry 5

I doubt not that since we are well persuaded we carry not a heart with us from hence that grows not in a fair consent with ours, nor leave not one behind that doth not wis success and conquest to attend on us

Cambridge

Never was monarch better feared and loved than is your majesty, there's not, I think, a subject that sits in heart-grief and uneasiness under the sweet shade of your government.

Grey

True: those that were your father's enemies have steeped their galls in honey and do serve you with hearts create of duty and of zeal.

King Henry 5

We therefore have great cause of thankfulness and shall forget the office of our hand, sooner than quittance of desert and merit according to the weight and worthiness.

Scroop

So service shall with steeled sinews toil, and labour shall refresh itself with hope to do your grace incessant services.

King Henry 5

We judge no less.

Uncle of Exeter, enlarge the man committed yesterday that railed against our person, we consider it was excess of wine that set him on and on his more advice we pardon him

Scroop

That's mercy, but too much security, let him be punished, sovereign, lest example breed by his sufferance, more of such a kind.

King Henry 5

Oh, let us yet be merciful.

Cambridge

So may your highness, and yet punis too.

Grey

Sir, you show great mercy, if you give him life after the taste of much correction.

King Henry 5

Alas, your too much love and care of me are heavy orisons against this poor wretch!

If little faults proceeding on distemper, shall not be winked at, how shall we stretch our eye when capital crimes are chewed, swallowed and digested,

Appear before us? We'll yet enlarge that man,

Though Cambridge, Scroop and Grey, in their dear care and tender preservation of our person, would have him punished.

And now to our French causes, who are the late commissioners?

Cambridge

I one, my lord

Your highness bade me ask for it to-day.

Scroop

So did you me, my liege.

Grey

And I, my royal sovereign.

King Henry 5

Then, Richard Earl of Cambridge, there is yours

There yours, Lord Scroop of Masham

And sir knight Grey of Northumberland, this same is yours, read them and know, I know your worthiness.

My Lord of Westmoreland, and uncle Exeter, we will aboard to night.

Why, how now, gentlemen!

What see you in those papers that you lose so much complexion?

Look ye, how they change!

Their cheeks are paper.

Why, what read you there that hath so cowarded and chased your blood out of appearance?

Cambridge

I do confess my fault

And do submit me to your highness' mercy.

Grey Scroop

To which we all appeal.

King Henry 5

The mercy that was quick in us but late by your own counsel is suppressed and killed, you must not dare, for shame, to talk of mercy

For your own reasons turn into your bosoms, as dogs upon their masters, worrying you. See you, my princes, and my noble peers, these Englis monsters!

My Lord of Cambridge here, you know how apt our love was to accord and furnis him with all appertinent belonging to his honour

This man hath, for a few light crowns, lightly conspired, and sworn unto the practises of France to kill us here in Hampton

To the which this knight, no less for bounty bound to us than Cambridge is, hath likewise sworn. But oh, what shall I say to thee, Lord Scroop?

Thou cruel, ingrateful, savage and inhuman creature!

Thou that didst bear the key of all my counsels that knew'st the very bottom of my soul, that almost mightst have coined me into gold, wouldst thou have practised on me for thy use?

May it be possible, that foreign hire could out of thee extract one spark of evil that might annoy my finger?

It is so strange, that though the truth of it stands off as gross as black and white, my eye will scarcely see it.

Treason and murder, ever kept together as two yoke-devils sworn to either's purpose, working so grossly in a natural cause that admiration did not whoop at them

But thou are against all proportion, did such bring in wonder to wait on treason and on murder?

And whatsoever cunning fiend it was that wrought upon thee so preposterously hath got the voice in hell for excellence

All other devils that suggest by treasons do botch and bungle up damnation with patches, colours, and with forms being fetched from glistering semblances of piety but he that tempered thee bade thee stand up, gave thee no instance why thou shouldst do treason, unless to dub thee with the name of traitor.

If that same demon that hath gulled thee thus should with his lion gait walk the whole world, he might return to vasty Tartar back and tell the legions 'I can never win a soul so easy as that Englishman's.'

Oh, how hast thou with 'jealousy infected the sweetness of affiance! Show men dutiful?

Why, so didst thou seem they grave and learned?

Why, so didst thou come they of noble family?

Why, so didst thou seem they religious?

Why, so didst thou or are they spare in diet,

Free from gross passion or of mirth or anger, constant in spirit, not swerving with the blood, garnished and decked in modest complement, not working with the eye without the ear, and but in purged judgment trusting neither?

Such and so finely bolted didst thou seem, and thus thy fall hath left a kind of blot to mark the full-fraught man and best induced with some suspicion.

I will weep for thee for this revolt of thine, methinks, is like another fall of man.

Their faults are open, arrest them to the answer of the law and God acquit them of their practises!

Exeter

I arrest thee of high treason, by the name of Richard Earl of Cambridge.

I arrest thee of high treason, by the name of Henry Lord Scroop of Masham.

I arrest thee of high treason, by the name of Thomas Grey, knight, of Northumberland.

Scroop

Our purposes God justly hath discovered and I repent my fault more than my death, which I beseech your highness to forgive, although my body pay the price of it.

Cambridge

For me the gold of France did not seduce

Although I did admit it as a motive the sooner to effect what I intended, but God be thanked for prevention, which I in sufferance heartily will rejoice, beseeching God and you to pardon me

Grey

Never did faithful subject more rejoice at the discovery of most dangerous treason than I do at this hour, with joy over myself.

Prevented from a damned enterprise, my fault, but not my body, pardon, sovereign

King Henry 5

God quit you in his mercy! Hear your sentence.

You have conspired against our royal person joined with an enemy proclaimed, and from his coffers received the golden earnest of our death

Wherein you would have sold your king to slaughter, his princes and his peers to servitude, his subjects to oppression and contempt and his whole kingdom into desolation

Touching our person seek we no revenge but we our kingdom's safety must so tender, whose ruin you have sought, that to her laws we do deliver you.

Get you therefore hence, poor miserable wretches, to your death, the taste whereof God of his mercy give you patience to endure, and true repentance of all your dear offences!

Bear them hence.

(Cambridge, Scroop and Grey exit, guarded)

Now, lords, for France; the enterprise whereof shall be to you, as us, like glorious.

We doubt not of a fair and lucky war since God so graciously hath brought to light this dangerous treason lurking in our way to hinder our beginnings.

We doubt not now but every rub is smoothed on our way.

Then forth, dear countrymen, let us deliver our puissance into the hand of God, putting it straight in expedition.

Cheerly to sea; the signs of war advance, no king of England, if not king of France.

(Exit)

Act 2 Scene 3

London. Before a tavern.

(Pistol, Hostess, NYM, Bardolph, and Boy enter)

Hostess

Pray I to thee, honey-sweet husband, let me bring thee to Staines.

Pistol

No, for my manly heart doth yearn.

Bardolph, be blithe

Nym, rouse thy vaunting veins

Boy, bristle thy courage up; for Falstaff he is dead, and we must yearn therefore.

Bardolph

Would I were with him, wheresomever he is, either in heaven or in hell!

Hostess

Nay, sure, he's not in hell: he's in Arthur's bosom, if ever man went to Arthur's bosom. ALL made a finer end and went away and it had been any christom child; all parted even just between twelve and one, even at the turning on the tide; for after I saw him fumble with the sheets and play with flowers and smile upon his fingers' ends, I knew there was but one way.

For his nose was as sharp as a pen, and all babbled of green fields. 'How now, sir John!' quoth I 'what, man! be of good cheer.'

So all cried out 'God, God, God!' three or four times.

Now I, to comfort him, bid him as should I, not thinking of God; I hoped there was no need to trouble himself with any such thoughts yet.

So all bade me lay more clothes on his feet, I put my hand into the bed and felt them, and they were as cold as any stone; then I felt to his knees and they were as cold as any stone, and so upward and upward, and all was as cold as any stone.

NYM

They say he cried out of sack.

Hostess

Ay, that all did.

Bardolph

And of women.

Hostess

Nay, that all did not.

Boy

Yes, that all did; and said they were devils incarnate.

Hostess

All could never abide carnation, it was a colour he never liked.

Boy

All said once, the devil would have him about women.

Hostess

All did in some sort, indeed, handle women, but then he was rheumatic, and talked of the whore of Babylon.

Boy

Do you not remember, all saw a flea stick upon Bardolph's nose, and all said it was a black soul burning in hell-fire?

Bardolph

Well, the fuel is gone that maintained that fire, that's all the riches I got in his service.

NYM

Shall we shog? The king will be gone from Southampton.

Pistol

Come, let's away. My love, give me thy lips.

Look to my chattels and my movables, let senses rule; the word is 'Pitch and Pay, trust none for oaths are straws, men's faiths are wafer-cakes, and hold-fast is the only dog, my duck.

Therefore, Caveto be thy counsellor.

Go, clear thy crystals. Yoke-fellows in arms, let us to France; like horse-leeches, my boys, to suck, to suck, the very blood to suck!

Boy

And that's but unwholesome food they say.

Pistol

Touch her soft mouth, and march.

Bardolph

Farewell, hostess.

(Kisses her)

NYM

I cannot kiss, that is the humour of it; but, adieu.

Pistol

Let housewifery appear, keep close, I thee command.

Hostess

Farewell; adieu.

(Exit)

Act 2 Scene 4

France. The King's palace.

Flourish.

(The French King, the Dauphin, the Dukes of Berri and Bretagne, the Constable, and others enter)

King of France

Thus comes the Englis with full power upon us, and more than carefully it us concerns to answer royally in our defences.

Therefore the Dukes of Berri and of Bretagne, of Brabant and of Orleans, shall make forth and you Prince Dauphin, with all swift dispatch to line and new repair our towns of war with men of courage and with means defendant.

For England his approaches makes as fierce as waters to the sucking of a gulf.

It fits us then to be as provident as fear may teach us out of late examples left by the fatal and neglected Englis upon our fields.

Dauphin

My most redoubted father, it is most meet we arm us against the foe, for peace itself should not so dull a kingdom, though war nor no known quarrel were in question.

But that defences, musters, preparations, should be maintained, assembled and collected, as were a war in expectation.

Therefore, I say it is meet we all go forth to view the sick and feeble parts of France, and let us do it with no show of fear. No, with no more than if we heard that England were busied with a Whitsun morris-dance.

For, my good liege, she is so idly kinged, her sceptre so fantastically borne by a vain, giddy, shallow, humorous youth, that fear attends her not.

Constable

Oh peace, Prince Dauphin!

You are too much mistaken in this king; question your grace the late ambassadors, with what great state he heard their embassy, how well supplied with noble counsellors, how modest in exception, and withal, how terrible in constant resolution.

You shall find his vanities forespent were but the outside of the Roman Brutus, covering discretion with a coat of folly; as gardeners do with ordure hide those roots that shall first spring and be most delicate.

Dauphin

Well, it is not so, my lord high constable, but though we think it so, it is no matter.

In cases of defence it is best to weigh the enemy more mighty than he seems

So the proportions of defence are filled, which of a weak or loathsome projection doth, like a miser, spoil his coat with scanting a little cloth.

King of France

Think we King Harry strong, and princes look you strongly arm to meet him.

The kindred of him hath been fleshed upon us and he is bred out of that bloody strain that haunted us in our familiar paths

Witness our too much memorable shame when Cressy battle fatally was struck, and all our princes captived by the hand of that black name, Edward, Black Prince of Wales

Whiles that his mountain sire, on mountain standing, up in the air crowned with the golden sun, saw his heroical seed and smiled to see him; mangle the work of nature and deface the patterns that by God and by French fathers had twenty years been made.

This is a stem of that victorious stock; and let us fear the native mightiness and fate of him.

(A Messenger enters)

Messenger

Ambassadors from Harry King of England

Do crave admittance to your majesty.

King of France

We'll give them present audience. Go, and bring them.

(Messenger and certain Lords exit)

You see this chase is hotly followed, friends.

Dauphin

Turn head and stop pursuit, for coward dogs most spend their mouths when what they seem to threaten runs far before them.

Good my sovereign, take up the Englis short, and let them know of what a monarchy you are the head

Self-love, my liege, is not so vile a sin as self-neglecting.

(Lords, with Exeter and train re-enter)

King of France

From our brother England?

Exeter

From him

He greets your majesty.

He wills you, in the name of God Almighty, that you divest yourself and lay apart the borrow'd glories that by gift of heaven by law of nature and of nations, along to him and to his heirs.

Namely, the crown and all wide-stretched honours that pertain by custom and the ordinance of times unto the crown of France

That you may know it is no sinister nor no awkward claim, picked from the worm-holes of long-vanished days, nor from the dust of old oblivion raked, he sends you this most memorable line

In every branch truly demonstrative, willing to overlook this pedigree, and when you find him evenly derived from his most famed of famous ancestors, Edward the Third.

He bids you then resign your crown and kingdom, indirectly held from him the native and true challenger.

King of France

Or else what follows?

Exeter

Bloody constraint, for if you hide the crown even in your hearts there will he rake for it

Therefore in fierce tempest is he coming, in thunder and in earthquake, like a Jupiter, that if requiring fail, he will compel

And bids you, in the bowels of the Lord, deliver up the crown and to take mercy on the poor souls for whom this hungry war opens his vasty jaws; and on your head

Turning the widows' tears, the orphans' cries the dead men's blood, the pining maidens groans for husbands. Fathers and betrothed lovers that shall be swallowed in this controversy

This is his claim, his threatening and my message, unless the Dauphin be in presence here, to whom expressly I bring greeting too.

King of France

For us, we will consider of this further

To-morrow shall you bear our full intent back to our brother England.

Dauphin, for the Dauphin, I stand here for him

What to him from England?

Exeter

Scorn and defiance; slight regard, contempt, and anything that may not misbecome the mighty sender, doth he prize you at.

Thus says my king, and if your father's highness do not, in grant of all demands at large, sweeten the bitter mock you sent his majesty; he'll call you to so hot an answer of it that caves and womby vaultages of France shall chide your trespass and return your mock in second accent of his ordnance.

Dauphin

Say, if my father render fair return, it is against my will; for I desire nothing but odds with England

To that end, as matching to his youth and vanity, I did present him with the Paris balls.

Exeter

He'll make your Paris Louvre shake for it, were it the mistress-court of mighty Europe

Be assured, you'll find a difference, as we his subjects have in wonder found between the promise of his greener days, and these he masters now

Now he weighs time even to the utmost grain

That you shall read in your own losses, if he stay in France.

King of France

To-morrow shall you know our mind at full.

Exeter

Dispatch us with all speed, lest that our king come here himself to question our delay. for he is footed in this land already.

King of France

You shall be soon dispatch's with fair conditions

A night is but small breath and little pause to answer matters of this consequence.

(Flourish)

(Exit)

Act 3 Intro

(Chorus enter)

Chorus

Thus with imagined wing our swift scene flies in motion of no less celerity than that of thought. Suppose that you have seen the well-appointed king at Hampton pier embark his royalty; and his brave fleet with silken streamers the young Phoebus fanning

Play with your fancies, and in them behold upon the hempen tackle ship-boys climbing

Hear the shrill whistle which doth order give to sounds confused; behold the threaden sails, borne with the invisible and creeping wind, draw the huge bottoms through the furrowed sea, breasting the lofty surge

Oh, do but think you stand upon the ravage and behold a city on the inconstant billows dancing

For so appears this fleet majestical, holding due course to Harfleur

Follow, follow

Grapple your minds to sternage of this navy and leave your England, as dead midnight still, guarded with grandsires, babies and old women; either past or not arrived to pith and puissance

For who is he, whose chin is but enriched with one appearing hair, that will not follow these cull'd and choice-drawn cavaliers to France?

Work, work your thoughts, and therein see a siege

Behold the ordnance on their carriages with fatal mouths gaping on girded Harfleur.

Suppose the ambassador from the French comes back

Tells Harry that the king doth offer him Katharine his daughter, and with her, to dowry, some petty and unprofitable dukedoms.

The offer likes not: and the nimble gunner with linstock now the devilis cannon touches,

(Alarum)

(Chambers go off)

And down goes all before them. Still be kind, and take out our performance with your mind.

(Exit)

Act 3 Scene 1

France. Before Harfleur.

Alarum.

(King Henry, Exeter, Bedford, Gloucester, and Soldiers enter with scaling-ladders)

King Henry 5

Once more unto the breach, dear friends, once more

Or close the wall up with our Englis dead. In peace there's nothing so becomes a man as modest stillness and humility

When the blast of war blows in our ears, then imitate the action of the tiger

Stiffen the sinews, summon up the blood, disguise fair nature with hard-favoured rage

Then lend the eye a terrible aspect

Let pry through the portage of the head like the brass cannon

Let the brow overwhelm it as fearfully as doth a galled rock overhang and jutty his confounded base, willed with the wild and wasteful ocean.

Now set the teeth and stretch the nostril wide, hold hard the breath and bend up every spirit to his full height.

On, on, you noblest English, whose blood is fet from fathers of war-proof!

Fathers that, like so many Alexanders have in these parts from morn till even fought and sheathed their swords for lack of argument

Dishonour not your mothers

Now attest that those whom you called fathers did beget you.

Be copy now to men of grosser blood and teach them how to war. And you good yeoman, whose limbs were made in England, show us here the mettle of your pasture.

Let us swear that you are worth your breeding

Which I doubt not

For there is none of you so mean and base that hath not noble lustre in your eyes

I see you stand like greyhounds in the slips, straining upon the start. The game's afoot

Follow your spirit, and upon this charge cry 'God for Harry, England, and Saint George!'

(Exit)

Alarum

(Chambers go off)

Act 3 Scene 2

France.

(NYM, Bardolph, Pistol, and Boy enter)

Bardolph

On, on, on, on, on! to the breach, to the breach!

NYM

I pray thee, corporal, stay

The knocks are too hot

For mine own part, I have not a case of lives

The humour of it is too hot, that is the very plain-song of it.

Pistol

The plain-song is most just: for humours do abound

Knocks go and come, God's vassals drop and die, and sword and shield in bloody field; doth win immortal fame.

Boy

Would I were in an alehouse in London! I would give all my fame for a pot of ale and safety.

Pistol

And I

If wishes would prevail with me, my purpose should not fail with me, but thither would I lie.

Boy

As duly, but not as truly, as bird doth sing on bough.

(Fluellen enters)

Fluellen

Up to the breach, you dogs! Forward, you cullions!

(Driving them forward)

Pistol

Be merciful, great duke, to men of mould.

Abate thy rage, abate thy manly rage, abate thy rage, great duke!

Good bawcock, bate thy rage; use lenity, sweet chuck!

NYM

These be good humours! your honour wins bad humours.

(All but Boy exit)

Boy

As young as I am, I have observed these three swashers. I am boy to them all three

All they three, though they would serve me, could not be man to me

For indeed three such antics do not amount to a man. For Bardolph, he is white-livered and red-faced

By the means whereof all faces it out, but fights not. For Pistol, he hath a killing tongue and a quiet sword

By the means whereof all breaks words, and keeps whole weapons. For Nym, he hath heard that men of few words are the best men

He scorns to say his prayers, lest all should be thought a coward

His few bad words are matched with as few good deeds

For all never broke any man's head but his own, and that was against a post when he was drunk.

They will steal anything, and call it purchase. Bardolph stole a lute-case, bore it twelve leagues, and sold it for three half pence.

Nym and Bardolph are sworn brothers in filching, and in Calais they stole a fire-shovel

I knew by that piece of service the men would carry coals they would have me as familiar with men's pockets as their gloves or their handkerchers

Which makes much against my manhood, if I should take from another's pocket to put into mine, for it is plain pocketing up of wrongs.

I must leave them, and seek some better service, their villany goes against my weak stomach and therefore I must cast it up.

(Exit)

(Fluellen re-enters with Gower following)

Gower

Captain Fluellen, you must come presently to the mines, the Duke of Gloucester would speak with you.

Fluellen

To the mines! tell you the duke, it is not so good to come to the mines

For, look you, the mines is not according to the disciplines of the war

The concavities of it is not sufficient

For, look you, the athversary, you may discuss unto the duke, look you, is digt himself four yard under the countermines

By Cheshu, I think all will plough up all, if there is not better directions.

Gower

The Duke of Gloucester, to whom the order of the siege is given, is altogether directed by an Irishman, a very valiant gentleman, in faith.

Fluellen

It is Captain Macmorris, is it not?

Gower

I think it be.

Fluellen

By Cheshu, he is an ass, as in the world

I will verify as much in his beard: be has no more directions in the true disciplines of the wars, look you, of the Roman disciplines, than is a puppy-dog.

(Macmorris and Captain Jamy enter)

Gower

Here all comes; and the Scots captain, Captain Jamy, with him.

Fluellen

Captain Jamy is a marvellous falourous gentleman, that is certain; and of great expedition and knowledge in the ancient wars are upon my particular knowledge of his directions

By Cheshu, he will maintain his argument as well as any military man in the world, in the disciplines of the pristine wars of the Romans.

Jamy

I say good-day, Captain Fluellen.

Fluellen

God-den to your worship, good Captain James.

Gower

How now, Captain Macmorris! have you quit the

mines? have the pioneers given over?

Macmorris

By Chrish, la! it is ill done

The work is give over, the trompet sound the retreat. By my hand, I swear, and my father's soul, the work is, will be done, is over

I would have blowed up the town, so Christ save me, la! In an hour: Oh, it is ill done, it is ill done; by my hand, it is ill done!

Fluellen

Captain Macmorris, I beseech you now, will you

voutsafe me, look you, a few disputations with you, as partly touching or concerning the disciplines of the war, the Roman wars, in the way of argument look you to friendly communication

Partly to satisfy my opinion, and partly for the satisfaction, look you of my mind as touching the direction of the military discipline

That is the point.

Jamy

It shall be vary god, good faith, good captains bath

I shall quit you with good leave, as I may pick occasion; that shall I, marry.

Macmorris

It is no time to discourse, so Christ save me

The day is hot, and the weather, and the wars, and the king, and the dukes

It is no time to discourse. The town is beseeched, and the trumpet call us to the breach

We talk, and be Christ do nothing

It is shame for us all

So God shall me, it is shame to stand still it is shame, by my hand

There is throats to be cut, and works to be done

If there is nothing done, so Christ shall also love me, la!

Jamy

By the mess, were these eyes of mine take themselves to slumber, I'll do good service, or I'll look in the ground for it

I, or go to death

And I'll pay, it as valorously as I may, that shall I surely do, that is the brief and the long. Marry, I would full fain hear some question between you to way.

Fluellen

Captain Macmorris, I think, look you, under your

correction, there is not many of your nation…

Macmorris

Of my nation! What is my nation? Is a villain and a bastard and a knave, and a rascal.

What is my nation? Who talks of my nation?

Fluellen

Look you, if you take the matter otherwise than is meant, Captain Macmorris, peradventure I shall think you do not use me with that affability as in discretion you ought to use me, look you.

Being as good a man as yourself, both in the disciplines of war, and in the derivation of my birth, and in other particularities

Macmorris

I do not know you so good a man as myself

So Christ save me, I will cut off your head.

Gower

Gentlemen both, you will mistake each other.

Jamy

A! that's a foul fault.

A parley sounded

Gower

The town sounds a parley.

Fluellen

Captain Macmorris, when there is more better opportunity to be required, look you, I will be so bold as to tell you I know the disciplines of war

There is an end.

(Exit)

Act 3 Scene 3

Before the gates.

The Governor and some Citizens on the walls; the Englis forces below. Enter King Henry and his train

King Henry 5

How yet resolves the governor of the town?

This is the latest speaking we will admit

Therefore to our best mercy give yourselves

Or like to men proud of destruction, defy us to our worst

For, as I am a soldier, a name that in my thoughts becomes me best if; I begin the battery once again I will not leave the half-achieved Harfleur till in her ashes she lie buried.

The gates of mercy shall be all shut up, and the fleshed soldier, rough and hard of heart, in liberty of bloody hand shall range with conscience wide as hell, mowing like grass, your fresh-fair virgins and your flowering infants.

What is it then to me, if impious war, arrayed in flames like to the prince of fiends

Do, with his smirched complexion, all fell feats enlinked to waste and desolation?

What is it to me, when you yourselves are cause, if your pure maidens fall into the hand of hot and forcing violation?

What rein can hold licentious wickedness when down the hill he holds his fierce career?

We may as bootless spend our vain command upon the enraged soldiers in their spoil as send precepts to the leviathan to come ashore

Therefore, you men of Harfleur, take pity of your town and of your people whiles yet my soldiers are in my command

Whiles yet the cool and temperate wind of grace overblows the filthy and contagious clouds of heady murder, spoil and villainy. If not, why, in a moment look to see the blind and bloody soldier with foul hand defile the locks of your shrill-shrieking daughters

Your fathers taken by the silver beards, and their most reverend heads dashed to the walls your naked infants spitted upon pikes, whiles the mad mothers with their howls confused

Do break the clouds, as did the wives of Jewry at Herod's bloody-hunting slaughtermen.

What say you? will you yield, and this avoid, or, guilty in defence, be thus destroyed?

Governor

Our expectation hath this day an end

The Dauphin, whom of succors we entreated, returns us that his powers are yet not ready to raise so great a siege.

Therefore, great king, we yield our town and lives to thy soft mercy.

Enter our gates; dispose of us and ours

For we no longer are defensible.

King Henry 5

Open your gates. Come, uncle Exeter, go you and enter Harfleur

There remain, and fortify it strongly against the French

Use mercy to them all. For us, dear uncle, the winter coming on and sickness growing upon our soldiers, we will retire to Calais. To-night in Harfleur we will be your guest

To-morrow for the march are we addrest.

Flourish.

(The King and his train enter the town)

Act 3 Scene 4

The French King's palace.

(Katharine and Alice enter)

Katharine

Alice, You have been to England, and you talk well the language.

Alice

A skin, madame.

Katharine

I pray to thee, teach me, I must learn. How-do you name this (points to hand) is English?

Alice

A hand ? That is called a hand.

Katharine

A hand. And what of these ? (Points towards fingers)

Alice

The fingers ? My faith, I forget what the each finger is named, though I shall remember. Together, they are called fingers

Katharine

The hand is this (points to hand) and the fingers are these (points to fingers). I think I am well schooled, I have learnt these words quickly. And what of this? (Points to the nail)

Comment appelez-vous les ongles?

Alice

The nail? These are called nails

Katharine

Naills, listen me, say to be if I speak well, hand! fingers! and nail!

De nails. Ecoutez; dites-moi, si je parle bien: de

Alice

You speak well, madamn, a very strong English

Katharine

What is this (Points to arms)

Alice

The arm, madame.

Katharine

(Points to elbow) This?

Alice

The elbow.

Katharine

The elbow. I will saw all the words I learn

Alice

It's too difficult madame, as I think it

Katharine

Excuse-moi, Alive, listen, the hand, the finger, the nail, the arm, the bell-bow

Alice

The elbow, madame.

Katharine

Oh dear Lord God! I forget the elbow!

And what of this? (points to neck)

Alice

The neck, madame.

Katharine

The nick. And this? (points to chin)?

Alice

The chin.

Katharine

The sin. The nick and the sin.

Alice

Yes, except your honour, in truth you pronounce as well as a native English !

Katharine

I learn, by the grace of God, I learn quickly

Alice

Have you not already forgotten of what I say

Katharine

No, I will repeat as you prompt, the hand, the fingers, a nails…

Alice

The nails, madame.

Katharine

The nails, the arm, the billbow.

Alice

Save your honor, the elbow

Katharine

As I say, the elbow, and the sin (points to chin). How you call this? (points to foot, shows her robe)

Alice

The foot, madame; and a robe.

Katharine

The foot and the robe! Oh lord God! These are words, of bad, currupted, large! shameless and for a woman of honour to use. I would not pronounce these words near French nobles of France, not for all the world

The foot and the robe

Well, let us repeat one more time, my lesson together : the hand, the fingers, the nails, the arm, the elbow, the nick, the sin, the robe

Alice

Excellent, madame!

Katharine

It is enough new words for this time, we will go dine

(Exit)

Act 3 Scene 5

The French King's palace.

(The King of France, the Dauphin, the Duke of Bourbon, the Constable of France, and others enter)

King of France

It is certain he hath passed the river Somme.

Constable

And if he be not fought withal, my lord, let us not live in France

Let us quit all and give our vineyards to a barbarous people.

Dauphin

Oh Living God! Ahall a few sprays of us, the emptying of our fathers' luxury, our scions put in wild and savage stock, spirit up so suddenly into the clouds, and overlook their grafters?

Bourbon

Normans, but bastard Normans, Norman bastards!

The death of me! If they march along

Unfought withal, but I will sell my dukedom to buy a slobbery and a dirty farm in that nook-shotten isle of Albion.

Constable

Oh God of War! Where have they this mettle?

Is not their climate foggy, raw and dull on whom, as in despite, the sun looks pale,

Killing their fruit with frowns? Can sodden water, a drench for surrendered jades, their barley-broth, decoct their cold blood to such valiant heat?

Shall our quick blood, spirited with wine, seem frosty?

Oh, for honour of our land, let us not hang like roping icicles upon our houses' thatch, whiles a more frosty people sweat drops of gallant youth in our rich fields!

Poor we may call them in their native lords.

Dauphin

By faith and honour, our madams mock at us, and plainly say our mettle is bred out and they will give their bodies to the lust of Englis youth to new-store France with bastard warriors.

Bourbon

They bid us to the English dancing-schools, and teach lavoltas high and swift corantos

Saying our grace is only in our heels and that we are most lofty runaways.

King of France

Where is Montjoy the herald? Speed him hence, let him greet England with our sharp defiance.

Up, princes! and, with spirit of honour edged more sharper than your swords, their to the field, Charles Delabreth, high constable of France

You Dukes of Orleans, Bourbon, and of Berri, Alencon, Brabant, Bar, and Burgundy

Jaques Chatillon, Rambures, Vaudemont, Beaumont, Grandpre, Roussi, and Fauconberg…

Foix, Lestrale, Bouciqualt, and Charolois

High dukes, great princes, barons, lords and knights, for your great seats now quit you of great shames.

Bar Harry England, that sweeps through our land with pennons painted in the blood of Harfleur, rush on his host, as doth the melted snow upon the valleys, whose low vassal seat the Alps doth spit and void his rheum upon

Go down upon him, you have power enough, and in a captive chariot into Rouen, bring him our prisoner.

Constable

This becomes the great.

Sorry am I his numbers are so few, his soldiers sick and famished in their march, for I am sure, when he shall see our army

He'll drop his heart into the sink of fear and for achievement offer us his ransom.

King of France

Therefore, lord constable, haste on Montjoy and let him say to England that we send to know what willing ransom he will give.

Prince Dauphin, you shall stay with us in Rouen.

Dauphin

Not so, I do beseech your majesty.

King of France

Be patient, for you shall remain with us.

Now forth, lord constable and princes all and quickly bring us word of England's fall.

(Exit)

Act 3 Scene 6

The English camp in Picardy.

(Gower and Fluellen enter, meeting)

Gower

How now, Captain Fluellen! come you from the bridge?

Fluellen

I assure you, there is very excellent services committed at the bridge.

Gower

Is the Duke of Exeter safe?

Fluellen

The Duke of Exeter is as magnanimous as Agamemnon

A man that I love and honour with my soul, and my heart, and my duty, and my life, and my living, and my uttermost power

He is not-God be praised and blessed!--any hurt in the world; but keeps the bridge most valiantly, with excellent discipline.

There is an aunchient lieutenant there at the pridge, I think in my very conscience he is as valiant a man as Mark Antony

He is a man of no estimation in the world; but did see him do as gallant service.

Gower

What do you call him?

Fluellen

He is called Aunchient Pistol.

Gower

I know him not.

(Pistol enters)

Fluellen

Here is the man.

Pistol

Captain, I thee beseech to do me favours

The Duke of Exeter doth love thee well.

Fluellen

Ay, I praise God; and I have merited some love at his hands.

Pistol

Bardolph, a soldier, firm and sound of heart, and of buxom valour, hath, by cruel fate, and giddy Fortune's furious fickle wheel

That goddess blind that stands upon the rolling restless stone…

Fluellen

By your patience, Aunchient Pistol. Fortune is painted blind, with a muffler afore her eyes, to signify to you that Fortune is blind

She is painted also with a wheel, to signify to you, which is the moral of it, that she is turning, and inconstant, and mutability, and variation

Her foot, look you, is fixed upon a spherical stone, which rolls, and rolls, and rolls: in good truth, the poet makes a most excellent description of it

Fortune is an excellent moral.

Pistol

Fortune is Bardolph's foe, and frowns on him

For he hath stolen a pax, and hanged must all be

A damned death!

Let gallows gape for dog; let man go free and let not hemp his windpipe suffocate

Exeter hath given the doom of death for pox of little price.

Therefore, go speak: the duke will hear thy voice

Let not Bardolph's vital thread be cut with edge of penny cord and vile reproach

Speak, captain, for his life, and I will thee requite.

Fluellen

Aunchient Pistol, I do partly understand your meaning.

Pistol

Why then, rejoice therefore.

Fluellen

Certainly, aunchient, it is not a thing to rejoice at

For if, look you, he were my brother, I would desire the duke to use his good pleasure, and put him to execution; for discipline ought to be used.

Pistol

Die and be damned! and figo for thy friendship!

Fluellen

It is well.

Pistol

The fig of Spain!

(Exit)

Fluellen

Very good.

Gower

Why, this is an arrant counterfeit rascal

I remember him now; a bawd, a cutpurse.

Fluellen

I'll assure you, all uttered as brave words at the bridge as you shall see in a summer's day.

It is very well; what he has spoke to me, that is well, I warrant you, when time is serve.

Gower

Why, it is a gull, a fool, a rogue, that now and then goes to the wars, to grace himself at his return into London under the form of a soldier.

Such fellows are perfect in the great commanders' names, and they will learn you by rote where services were

Done

At such and such a sconce, at such a breach, at such a convoy who came off bravely, who was shot, who disgraced what terms the enemy stood on

This they con perfectly in the phrase of war, which they trick up with new-tuned oaths

What a beard of the general's cut and a horrid suit of the camp will do among foaming bottles and ale-washed wits, is wonderful to be thought on.

You must learn to know such slanders of the age, or else you may be marvellously mistook.

Fluellen

I tell you what, Captain Gower; I do perceive he is not the man that he would gladly make show to the world he is

If I find a hole in his coat, I will tell him my mind.

(Drum heard)

Hark you, the king is coming, and I must speak with him from the pridge.

(Drum and colours)

(King Henry, Gloucester, and Soldiers enter)

God pless your majesty!

King Henry 5

How now, Fluellen! camest thou from the bridge?

Fluellen

Ay, so please your majesty.

The Duke of Exeter has very gallantly maintained the bridge.

The French is gone off, look you

There is gallant and most brave passages; marry, that adversary was have possession of the bridge

He is enforced to retire, and the Duke of Exeter is master of the bridge

I can tell your majesty, the duke is a brave man.

King Henry 5

What men have you lost, Fluellen?

Fluellen

The perdition of that adversary hath been very great, reasonable great

Marry, for my part, I think the duke hath lost never a man, but one that is like to be executed for robbing a church

One Bardolph, if your majesty know the man

His face is all bubukles, and whelks, and knobs, and flames of fire

His lips blows at his nose, and it is like a coal of fire, sometimes blue and sometimes red

His nose is executed and his fire's out.

King Henry 5

We would have all such offenders so cut off: and we give express charge, that in our marches through the country, there be nothing compelled from the villages, nothing taken but paid for, none of the French upbraided or abused in disdainful language

For when lenity and cruelty play for a kingdom, the gentler gamester is the soonest winner.

(Montjoy enters)

Montjoy

You know me by my habit.

King Henry 5

Well then I know thee

What shall I know of thee?

Montjoy

My master's mind.

King Henry 5

Unfold it.

Montjoy

Thus says my king

Say thou to Harry of England

Though we seemed dead, we did but sleep

Advantage is a better soldier than rashness.

Tell him we could have rebuked him at Harfleur, but that we thought not good to bruise an injury till it were full ripe

Now we speak upon our cue, and our voice is imperial

England shall repent his folly, see his weakness, and admire our sufferance.

Bid him therefore consider of his ransom, which must proportion the losses we have borne, the subjects we have lost, the disgrace we have digested; which in weight to re-answer, his pettiness would bow under.

For our losses, his exchequer is too poor; for the effusion of our blood, the muster of his kingdom too faint a number; and for our disgrace, his own person, kneeling at our feet, but a weak and worthless satisfaction.

To this add defiance: and tell him, for conclusion, he hath betrayed his followers, whose condemnation is pronounced.

So far my king and master; so much my office.

King Henry 5

What is thy name? I know thy quality.

Montjoy

Montjoy.

King Henry 5

Thou dost thy office fairly.

Turn thee back and tell thy king I do not seek him now

Could be willing to march on to Calais without impeachment

For, to say the sooth, though it is no wisdom to confess so much unto an enemy of craft and vantage, my people are with sickness much enfeebled, my numbers lessened, and those few I have almost no better than so many French

Who when they were in health, I tell thee, herald, I thought upon one pair of English legs did march three Frenchmen.

Yet, forgive me, God, that I do brag thus! This your air of France hath blown that vice in me:

I must repent.

Go therefore, tell thy master here I am

My ransom is this frail and worthless trunk, my army but a weak and sickly guard

Yet, God before, tell him we will come on, though France himself and such another neighbor stand in our way.

There's for thy labour, Montjoy, go bid thy master well advise himself

If we may pass, we will; if we be hindered, Wee shall your tawny ground with your red blood discolour: and so Montjoy, fare you well.

The sum of all our answer is but this

We would not seek a battle, as we are

Nor, as we are, we say we will not shun it

So tell your master.

Montjoy

I shall deliver so.

Thanks to your highness.

(Exit)

Gloucester

I hope they will not come upon us now.

King Henry 5

We are in God's hand, brother, not in theirs.

March to the bridge

It now draws toward night

Beyond the river we'll encamp ourselves, and on to-morrow, bid them march away.

(Exit)

Act 3 Scene 7

The French camp, near Agincourt.

(The Constable of France, the LORD Rambures, Orleans, Dauphin, with others enter)

Constable

Tut! I have the best armour of the world.

Would it were day!

Orleans

You have an excellent armour, but let my horse have his due.

Constable

It is the best horse of Europe.

Orleans

Will it never be morning?

Dauphin

My lord of Orleans, and my lord high constable, you

talk of horse and armour?

Orleans

You are as well provided of both as any prince in the world.

Dauphin

What a long night is this! I will not change my horse with any that treads but on four pasterns.

Ca, ha! he bounds from the earth, as if his entrails were hairs

The flying horse, the Pegasus

To the nostrils of fire when I bestride him, I soar, I am a hawk

He trots the air

The earth sings when he touches it

The basest horn of his hoof is more musical than the pipe of Hermes.

Orleans

He's of the colour of the nutmeg.

Dauphin

And of the heat of the ginger.

It is a beast for Perseus

He is pure air and fire

The dull elements of earth and water never appear in him, but only in Patient stillness while his rider mounts him

He is indeed a horse

All other jades you may call beasts.

Constable

Indeed, my lord, it is a most absolute and excellent horse.

Dauphin

It is the prince of palfreys; his neigh is like the bidding of a monarch and his countenance enforces homage.

Orleans

No more, cousin.

Dauphin

Nay, the man hath no wit that cannot, from the rising of the lark to the lodging of the lamb, vary deserved praise on my palfrey.

It is a theme as fluent as the sea

Turn the sands into eloquent tongues, and my horse is argument for them all

It is a subject for a sovereign to reason on, and for a sovereign's sovereign to ride on

For the world, familiar to us and unknown to lay apart their particular functions and wonder at him

I once writ a sonnet in his praise and began thus, wonder of nature…

Orleans

I have heard a sonnet begin so to one's mistress.

Dauphin

Then did they imitate that which I composed to my courser, for my horse is my mistress.

Orleans

Your mistress bears well.

Dauphin

I am well, which is the prescript praise and perfection of a good and particular mistress.

Constable

Nay, for methought yesterday your mistress shrewdly shook your back.

Dauphin

So perhaps did yours.

Constable

Mine was not bridled.

Dauphin

Oh then belike she was old and gentle; and you rode, like a kern of Ireland, your French hose off, and in your straight trousers.

Constable

You have good judgment in horsemanship.

Dauphin

Be warned by me, then: they that ride so and ride not warily, fall into foul bogs.

I had rather have my horse to my mistress.

Constable

I had as belief have my mistress a jade.

Dauphin

I tell thee, constable, my mistress wears his own hair.

Constable

I could make as true a boast as that, if I had a sow to my mistress.

Dauphin

The dog is return to his proper vomiting, and the loath awakens, washes at the bog

Thou makest use of any thing.

Constable

Yet do I not use my horse for my mistress, or any such proverb so little kin to the purpose.

Rambures

My lord constable, the armour that I saw in your tent to-night, are those stars or suns upon it?

Constable

Stars, my lord.

Dauphin

Some of them will fall to-morrow, I hope.

Constable

And yet my sky shall not want.

Dauphin

That may be, for you bear a many superfluously, and it were more honour some were away.

Constable

Even as your horse bears your praises; who would trot as well, were some of your brags dismounted.

Dauphin

Would I were able to load him with his desert!

Will it never be day? I will trot to-morrow a mile, and my way shall be paved with English faces.

Constable

I will not say so, for fear I should be faced out of my way

I would it were morning

For I would fain be about the ears of the English.

Rambures

Who will go to hazard with me for twenty prisoners?

Constable

You must first go yourself to hazard, here you have them.

Dauphin

It is midnight

I'll go arm myself.

(Exit)

Orleans

The Dauphin longs for morning.

Rambures

He longs to eat the English.

Constable

I think he will eat all he kills.

Orleans

By the white hand of my lady, he's a gallant prince.

Constable

Swear by her foot, that she may tread out the oath.

Orleans

He is simply the most active gentleman of France.

Constable

Doing is activity; and he will still be doing.

Orleans

He never did harm, that I heard of.

Constable

Nor will do none to-morrow: he will keep that good name still.

Orleans

I know him to be valiant.

Constable

I was told that by one that knows him better than you.

Orleans

What's he?

Constable

Marry, he told me so himself; and he said he cared not who knew it

Orleans

He needs not

It is no hidden virtue in him.

Constable

By my faith, sir, but it is

Never any body saw it but his lackey

It is a hooded valour

When it appears, it will bate.

Orleans

Ill will never said well.

Constable

I will cap that proverb with 'There is flattery in friendship.'

Orleans

And I will take up that with 'Give the devil his due.'

Constable

Well placed: there stands your friend for the devil

Have at the very eye of that proverb with 'A pox of the devil.'

Orleans

You are the better at proverbs, by how much 'A fool's bolt is soon shot.'

Constable

You have shot over.

Orleans

It is not the first time you were overshot.

(A Messenger enters)

Messenger

My lord high constable, the English lie within fifteen hundred paces of your tents.

Constable

Who hath measured the ground?

Messenger

The Lord Grandpre.

Constable

A valiant and most expert gentleman.

Would it were day! Alas, poor Harry of England!

He longs not for the dawning as we do.

Orleans

What a wretched and peevis fellow is this king of England, to mope with his fat-brained followers so far out of his knowledge!

Constable

If the English had any apprehension, they would run away.

Orleans

That they lack

For if their heads had any intellectual armour, they could never wear such heavy head-pieces.

Rambures

That island of England breeds very valiant creatures; their mastiffs are of unmatchable courage.

Orleans

Foolish curs, that run winking into the mouth of a Russian bear and have their heads crushed like rotten apples!

You may as well say, that's a valiant flea that dare eat his breakfast on the lip of a lion.

Constable

Just, just

The men do sympathize with the mastiffs in robustious and rough coming on, leaving their wits with their wives

Then give them great meals of beef and iron and steel, they will eat like wolves and fight like devils.

Orleans

Ay, but these Englis are shrewdly out of beef.

Constable

Then shall we find to-morrow they have only stomachs to eat and none to fight.

Now is it time to arm

Come, shall we about it?

Orleans

It is now two o'clock: but, let me see, by ten we shall have each a hundred Englishmen.

(Exit)

Act 4 Intro

(Chorus enters)

Chorus

Now entertain conjecture of a time when creeping murmur and the poring dark fills the wide vessel of the universe.

From camp to camp through the foul womb of night

The hum of either army stilly sounds, that the fixed sentinels almost receive the secret whispers of each other's watch

Fire answers fire, and through their paly flames each battle sees the other's umbered face

Steed threatens steed, in high and boastful neighs piercing the night's dull ear, and from the tents the armourers, accomplishing the knights, with busy hammers closing rivets up, give dreadful note of preparation

The country cocks do crow, the clocks do toll, and the third hour of drowsy morning name.

Proud of their numbers and secure in soul, the confident and over-lusty French do the low-rated Englis play at dice

Chide the cripple tardy-gaited night who, like a foul and ugly witch, doth limp so tediously away.

The poor condemned English, like sacrifices, by their watchful fires sit patiently and inly ruminate the morning's danger, and their gesture sad investing lank-lean

Cheeks and war-worn coats presenteth them unto the gazing moon so many horrid ghosts.

Oh now, who will behold the royal captain of this ruined band walking from watch to watch, from tent to tent, let him cry 'Praise and glory on his head!'

For forth he goes and visits all his host.

Bids them good morrow with a modest smile and calls them brothers, friends and countrymen.

Upon his royal face there is no note how dread an army hath enrounded him

Nor doth he dedicate one jot of colour unto the weary and all-watched night, but freshly looks and over-bears attaint

With cheerful semblance and sweet majesty

That every wretch, pining and pale before, beholding him, plucks comfort from his looks

A largess universal like the sun his liberal eye doth give to every one, thawing cold fear, that mean and gentle all, behold, as may unworthiness define, a little touch of Harry in the night.

And so our scene must to the battle fly

Where--O for pity!--we shall much disgrace with four or five most vile and ragged foils, right ill-disposed in brawl ridiculous, the name of Agincourt.

Yet sit and see, minding true things by what their mockeries be.

(Exit)

Act 4 Scene 1

The English camp at Agincourt.

(King Henry, Bedford, and Gloucester enter)

King Henry 5

Gloucester, it is true that we are in great danger

The greater therefore should our courage be.

Good morrow, brother Bedford. God Almighty!

There is some soul of goodness in things evil, would men observingly distil it out.

For our bad neighbour makes us early stirrers, which is both healthful and good husbandry

Besides, they are our outward consciences, and preachers to us all, admonishing that we should dress us fairly for our end.

Thus may we gather honey from the weed, and make a moral of the devil himself.

(Erpingham enters)

Good morrow, old Sir Thomas Erpingham

A good soft pillow for that good white head were better than a churlis turf of France.

Erpingham

Not so, my liege: this lodging likes me better, since I may say 'Now lie I like a king.'

King Henry 5

It is good for men to love their present pains upon example; so the spirit is eased

When the mind is quickened, out of doubt, the organs, though defunct and dead before, break up their drowsy grave and newly move, with casted slough and fresh legerity.

Lend me thy cloak, Sir Thomas.

Brothers both, commend me to the princes in our camp

Do my good morrow to them, and anon desire them and to my pavilion.

Gloucester

We shall, my liege.

Erpingham

Shall I attend your grace?

King Henry 5

No, my good knight

Go with my brothers to my lords of England

I and my bosom must debate awhile, and then I would no other company.

Erpingham

The Lord in heaven bless thee, noble Harry!

(All exit but King Henry)

King Henry 5

God-a-mercy, old heart! thou speak'st cheerfully.

(Pistol enters)

Pistol

Who goes there?

King Henry 5

A friend.

Pistol

Discuss unto me; art thou officer?

Or art thou base, common and popular?

King Henry 5

I am a gentleman of a company.

Pistol

Trail'st thou the puissant pike?

King Henry 5

Even so. What are you?

Pistol

As good a gentleman as the emperor.

King Henry 5

Then you are a better than the king.

Pistol

The king's a bawcock, and a heart of gold, a lad of life, an imp of fame of parents good, of fist most valiant.

I kiss his dirty shoe, and from heart-string I love the lovely bully.

What is thy name?

King Henry 5

Harry le Roy.

Pistol

The King! a Cornis name: art thou of Cornis crew?

King Henry 5

No, I am a Welshman.

Pistol

Know'st thou Fluellen?

King Henry 5

Yes.

Pistol

Tell him, I'll knock his leek about his pate

Upon Saint Davy's day.

King Henry 5

Do not you wear your dagger in your cap that day, lest he knock that about yours.

Pistol

Art thou his friend?

King Henry 5

And his kinsman too.

Pistol

The figo for thee, then!

King Henry 5

I thank you: God be with you!

Pistol

My name is Pistol called.

(Exit)

King Henry 5

It sorts well with your fierceness.

(Fluellen and Gower enter)

Gower

Captain Fluellen!

Fluellen

So! in the name of Jesu Christ, speak lower.

It is the greatest admiration of the universal world, when the true and aunchient prerogatifes and laws of the wars is not kept

If you would take the pains but to examine the wars of Pompey the Great, you shall find, I warrant you, that there is no tiddle toddle nor pibble pabble in Pompey's camp

I warrant you, you shall find the ceremonies of the wars, and the cares of it, and the forms of it, and the sobriety of it, and the modesty of it, to be otherwise.

Gower

Why, the enemy is loud; you hear him all night.

Fluellen

If the enemy is an ass and a fool and a prating coxcomb, is it meet, think you, that we should also, look you, be an ass and a fool and a prating coxcomb? In your own conscience, now?

Gower

I will speak lower.

Fluellen

I pray you and beseech you that you will.

(Gower and Fluellen exit)

King Henry 5

Though it appear a little out of fashion,

There is much care and valour in this Welshman.

Three soldiers, John Bates, Alexander Court, and Michael Williams enter)

Court

Brother John Bates, is not that the morning which breaks yonder?

Bates

I think it be

We have no great cause to desire the approach of day.

Williams

We see yonder the beginning of the day, but I think we shall never see the end of it.

Who goes there?

King Henry 5

A friend.

Williams

Under what captain serve you?

King Henry 5

Under Sir Thomas Erpingham.

Williams

A good old commander and a most kind gentleman

I pray you, what thinks he of our estate?

King Henry 5

Even as men wrecked upon a sand, that look to be washed off the next tide.

Bates

He hath not told his thought to the king?

King Henry 5

No; nor it is not meet he should.

For, though I speak it to you, I think the king is but a man, as I am

The violet smells to him as it doth to me

The element shows to him as it doth to me

All his senses have but human conditions: his ceremonies laid by, in his nakedness he appears but a man

Though his affections are higher mounted than ours, yet, when they stoop, they stoop with the like wing.

Therefore when he sees reason of fears, as we do, his fears, out of doubt, be of the same relish as ours are: yet, in reason, no man should possess him with any appearance of fear, lest he, by showing it, should dishearten his army.

Bates

He may show what outward courage he will

I believe, as cold a night as 'tis, he could wish himself in Thames up to the neck

So I would he were, and I by him, at all adventures, so we were quit here.

King Henry 5

By my troth, I will speak my conscience of the king

I think he would not wish himself any where but where he is.

Bates

Then I would he were here alone; so should he be sure to be ransomed, and a many poor men's lives saved.

King Henry 5

I dare say you love him not so ill, to wish him here alone, howsoever you speak this to feel other men's minds

Methinks I could not die any where so contented as in the king's company

His cause being just and his quarrel honourable.

Williams

That's more than we know.

Bates

Ay, or more than we should seek after; for we know enough, if we know we are the kings subjects

If his cause be wrong, our obedience to the king wipes the crime of it out of us.

Williams

But if the cause be not good, the king himself hath a heavy reckoning to make, when all those legs and arms and heads, chopped off in battle, shall join together at the latter day and cry all, we died at such a place

Some swearing, some crying for a surgeon, some upon their wives left poor behind them, some upon the debts they owe, some upon their children rawly left.

I am afeard there are few die well that die in a battle

For how can they charitably dispose of any thing, when blood is their argument?

Now, if these men do not die well, it will be a black matter for the king that led them to it

To disobey were against all proportion of subjection.

King Henry 5

So, if a son that is by his father sent about merchandise do sinfully miscarry upon the sea, the imputation of his wickedness by your rule, should be imposed upon his father that sent him

If a servant, under his master's command transporting a sum of money, be assailed by robbers and die in many irreconciled iniquities, you may call the business of the master the author of the servant's damnation

This is not so

The king is not bound to answer the particular endings of his soldiers, the father of his son, nor the master of his servant

They purpose not their death, when they purpose their services.

Besides, there is no king, be his cause never so spotless, if it come to the arbitrement of swords, can try it out with all unspotted soldiers, some peradventure have on them the guilt of premeditated and contrived murder

Of beguiling virgins with the broken seals of perjury

Making the wars their bulwark, that have before gored the gentle bosom of peace with pillage and robbery.

Now, if these men have defeated the law and outrun native punishment, though they can outstrip men, they have no wings to fly from God.

War is his beadle, war is vengeance

So that here men are punished for before-breach of the king's laws in now the king's quarrel where they feared the death, they have borne life away

Where they would be safe, they perish, then if they die unprovided, no more is the king guilty of their damnation than he was before guilty of those impieties for the which they are now visited.

Every subject's duty is the king's

Every subject's soul is his own.

Therefore should every soldier in the wars do as every sick man in his bed, wash every mote out of his conscience

Dying so, death is to him advantage; or not dying, the time was blessedly lost wherein such preparation was gained

In him that escapes, it were not sin to think that, making God so free an offer, he let him outlive that day to see his greatness and to teach others how they should prepare.

Williams

It is certain, every man that dies ill, the ill upon his own head, the king is not to answer it.

Bates

But I do not desire he should answer for me

Yet, I determine to fight lustily for him.

King Henry 5

I myself heard the king say he would not be ransomed.

Williams

Ay, he said so, to make us fight cheerfully

When our throats are cut, he may be ransomed, and we never the wiser.

King Henry 5

If I live to see it, I will never trust his word after.

Williams

You pay him then. That's a perilous shot out of an elder-gun, that a poor and private displeasure can do against a monarch!

You may as well go about to turn the sun to ice with fanning in his face with a peacock's feather.

You'll never trust his word after!

Come, it is a foolish saying.

King Henry 5

Your reproof is something too round

I should be angry with you, if the time were convenient.

Williams

Let it be a quarrel between us, if you live.

King Henry 5

I embrace it.

Williams

How shall I know thee again?

King Henry 5

Give me any gage of thine, and I will wear it in my bonnet

Then, if ever thou darest acknowledge it, I will make it my quarrel.

Williams

Here's my glove: give me another of thine.

King Henry 5

There.

Williams

This will I also wear in my cap

If ever thou come to me and say, after to-morrow, this is my glove, by this hand I will take thee a box on the ear.

King Henry 5

If ever I live to see it, I will challenge it.

Williams

Thou darest as well be hanged.

King Henry 5

Well. I will do it, though I take thee in the king's company.

Williams

Keep thy word: fare thee well.

Bates

Be friends, you English fools, be friends: we have French quarrels are now, if you could tell how to reckon.

King Henry 5

Indeed, the French may lay twenty French crowns to one, they will beat us

They bear them on their shoulders, but it is no English treason to cut French crowns, and to-morrow the king himself will be a clipper.

(Soldiers exit)

Upon the king! let us our lives, our souls, our debts, our careful wives, our children and our sins lay on the king!

We must bear all. Oh hard condition, twin-born with greatness, subject to the breath of every fool, whose sense no more can feel but his own wringing! What infinite heart's-ease must kings neglect, that private men enjoy!

And what have kings, that privates have not too, save ceremony, save general ceremony?

And what art thou, thou idle ceremony?

What kind of god art thou, that suffer'st more of mortal griefs than do thy worshippers?

What are thy rents? what are thy comings in?

Oh ceremony, show me but thy worth!

What is thy soul of adoration?

Art thou aught else but place, degree and form, creating awe and fear in other men?

Wherein thou art less happy being feared than they in fearing what drink'st thou oft, instead of homage sweet, but poisoned flattery?

Oh be sick, great greatness and bid thy ceremony give thee cure!

Think'st thou the fiery fever will go out with titles blown from adulation?

Will it give place to flexure and low bending?

Canst thou, when thou command'st the beggar's knee, command the health of it?

No, thou proud dream, that play'st so subtly with a king's repose

I am a king that find thee, and I know it is not the balm, the sceptre and the ball, the sword, the mace, the crown imperial, the intertissued robe of gold and pearl, the farced title running before the king, the throne he sits on, nor the tide of pomp that beats upon the high shore of this world.

No, not all these, thrice-gorgeous ceremony, not all these, laid in bed majestical, can sleep so soundly as the wretched slave, who with a body filled and vacant mind gets him to rest, crammed with distressful bread never sees horrid night, the child of hell, but like a lackey, from the rise to set sweats in the eye of Phoebus and all night sleeps in Elysium

Next day after dawn, doth rise and help Hyperion to his horse, and follows so the ever-running year, with profitable labour, to his grave

But for ceremony, such a wretch, winding up days with toil and nights with sleep, had the fore-hand and vantage of a king. the slave, a member of the country's peace, enjoys it

In gross brain little wots what watch the king keeps to maintain the peace, whose hours the peasant best advantages.

(Erpingham enter)

Erpingham

My lord, your nobles, jealous of your absence, seek through your camp to find you.

King Henry 5

Good old knight, collect them all together at my tent

I'll be before thee.

Erpingham

I shall do it, my lord.

(Exit)

King Henry 5

Oh God of battles! steel my soldiers' hearts

Possess them not with fear

Take from them now the sense of reckoning, if the opposed numbers Pluck their hearts from them.

Not to-day, oh Lord, Oh not to-day, think not upon the fault my father made in compassing the crown!

I Richard's body have interred anew

On it have bestowed more contrite tears than from it issued forced drops of blood

Five hundred poor I have in yearly pay, who twice a-day their wither'd hands hold up toward heaven, to pardon blood

I have built two chantries, where the sad and solemn priests sing still for Richard's soul.

More will I do

Though all that I can do is nothing worth, since that my penitence comes after all, imploring pardon.

(Gloucester enters)

Gloucester

My liege!

King Henry 5

My brother Gloucester's voice?

Ay

I know thy errand, I will go with thee

The day, my friends and all things stay for me.

(Exit)

Act 4 Scene 2

The French camp.

(The Dauphin, Orleans, Rambures, and others enter)

Orleans

The sun doth gild our armour; up, my lords!

Dauphin

Montez A cheval! My horse! varlet! laquais! ha!

Orleans

Oh brave spirit!

Dauphin

Via! The waters and the earth.

Orleans

Nothing more? Air and fire.

Dauphin

Heavens, cousin Orleans.

(Constable enter)

Now, my lord constable!

Constable

Hark, how our steeds for present service neigh!

Dauphin

Mount them, and make incision in their hides, that their hot blood may spin in English eyes, and doubt them with superfluous courage, ha!

Rambures

What, will you have them weep our horses' blood?

How shall we, then, behold their natural tears?

(Messenger enters)

Messenger

The English are embattled, you French peers.

Constable

To horse, you gallant princes! straight to horse!

Do but behold yon poor and starved band and your fair show shall suck away their souls, leaving them but the shells and husks of men.

There is not work enough for all our hands

Scarce blood enough in all their sickly veins to give each naked curtle-axe a stain, that our French gallants shall to-day draw out, and sheathe for lack of sport

Let us but blow on them, the vapour of our valour will overturn them.

It is positive against all exceptions, lords, that our superfluous lackeys and our peasants, who in unnecessary action swarm about our squares of battle, were we now to purge this field of such a holding foe, though we upon this mountain's basis by Took stand for idle speculation:

But that our honours must not. What's to say?

A very little little let us do.

All is done. Then let the trumpets sound the tucket sonance and the note to mount

For our approach shall so much dare the field that England shall couch down in fear and yield.

(Grandpre enter)

Grandpre

Why do you stay so long, my lords of France?

Yon island carrions, desperate of their bones, Ill-favouredly become the morning field

Their ragged curtains poorly are let loose, and our air shakes them passing scornfully

Big Mars seems bankrupt in their beggar'd host and faintly through a rusty beaver peeps

The horsemen sit like fixed candlesticks, with torch-staves in their hand; and their poor jades lob down their heads, dropping the hides and hips, the gum down-roping from their pale-dead eyes and in their pale dull mouths the gimmal bit lies foul with chew'd grass, still and motionless

Their executors, the knavis crows, fly over them, all impatient for their hour.

Description cannot suit itself in words to demonstrate the life of such a battle in life so lifeless as it shows itself.

Constable

They have said their prayers, and they stay for death.

Dauphin

Shall we go send them dinners and fresh suits and give their fasting horses provender, and after fight with them?

Constable

I stay but for my guidon: to the field!

I will the banner from a trumpet take, and use it for my haste. Come, come, away!

The sun is high, and we outwear the day.

(Exits)

Act 4 Scene 3

The English camp.

(Gloucester, Bedford, Exeter, Erpingham, with all his host: Salisbury and Westmoreland enter)

Gloucester

Where is the king?

Bedford

The king himself is rode to view their battle.

Westmoreland

Of fighting men they have full three score thousand.

Exeter

There's five to one; besides, they all are fresh.

Salisbury

God's arm strike with us! it is a fearful odds.

God be win you, princes all

I'll to my charge

If we no more meet till we meet in heaven, then, joyfully, my noble Lord of Bedford, my dear Lord Gloucester, and my good Lord Exeter, and my kind kinsman, warriors all, adieu!

Bedford

Farewell, good Salisbury; and good luck go with thee!

Exeter

Farewell, kind lord; fight valiantly to-day

Yet I do thee wrong to mind thee of it, for thou art framed of the firm truth of valour.

(Salisbury exits)

Bedford

He is full of valour as of kindness;

Princely in both.

(The King enters)

Westmoreland

Oh that we now had here but one ten thousand of those men in England that do no work to-day!

King Henry 5

What's he that wishes so?

My cousin Westmoreland? No, my fair cousin

If we are marked to die, we are we now to do our country loss; and if to live, the fewer men, the greater share of honour. God's will!

I pray thee, wish not one man more.

By Jupiter, I am not covetous for gold, nor care I who doth feed upon my cost

It yearns me not if men my garments wear

Such outward things dwell not in my desires, but if it be a sin to covet honour, I am the most offending soul alive.

No, faith, my coz, wish not a man from England, God's peace!

I would not lose so great an honour as one man more, methinks, would share from me for the best hope I have.

Oh, do not wis one more!

Rather proclaim it, Westmoreland, through my host, that he which hath no stomach to this fight, let him depart

His passport shall be made and crowns for convoy put into his purse

We would not die in that man's company that fears his fellowship to die with us.

This day is called the feast of Crispian, he that outlives this day, and comes safe home,

Will stand a tip-toe when the day is named, and rouse him at the name of Crispian.

He that shall live this day, and see old age, will yearly on the vigil feast his neighbours, and say 'To-morrow is Saint Crispian'

Then will he strip his sleeve and show his scars.

Say 'These wounds I had on Crispin's day.' Old men forget: yet all shall be forgot, but he'll remember with advantages what feats he did that day: then shall our names.

Familiar in his mouth as household words Harry the king, Bedford and Exeter, Warwick and Talbot, Salisbury and Gloucester, be in their flowing cups freshly remembered.

This story shall the good man teach his son

Crispin Crispian shall never go by from this day to the ending of the world, but we in it shall be remembered

We few, we happy few, we band of brothers

For he to-day that sheds his blood with me shall be my brother

Be he never so vile, this day shall gentle his condition, and gentlemen in England now a-bed shall think themselves accursed they were not here, and hold their manhoods cheap whiles any speaks that fought with us upon Saint Crispin's day.

(Salisbury re-enters)

Salisbury

My sovereign lord, bestow yourself with speed

The French are bravely in their battles set, and will with all expedience charge on us.

King Henry 5

All things are ready, if our minds be so.

Westmoreland

Perish the man whose mind is backward now!

King Henry 5

Thou does not wish more help from England, coz?

Westmoreland

God's will! my liege, would you and I alone, without more help, could fight this royal battle!

King Henry 5

Why, now thou hast unwished five thousand men

Which likes me better than to wis us one.

You know your places, God be with you all!

(Tucket)

(Montjoy enters)

Montjoy

Once more I come to know of thee, King Harry, if for thy ransom thou wilt now compound, before thy most assured overthrow, for certainly thou art so near the gulf, thou needs must be englutted.

Besides, in mercy, the constable desires thee thou wilt mind thy followers of repentance

That their souls may make a peaceful and a sweet retire from off these fields, where, wretches, their poor bodies must lie and fester.

King Henry 5

Who hath sent thee now?

Montjoy

The Constable of France.

King Henry 5

I pray thee, bear my former answer back, bid them achieve me and then sell my bones.

Good God! why should they mock poor fellows thus?

The man that once did sell the lion's skin while the beast lived, was killed with hunting him.

A many of our bodies shall no doubt find native graves; upon the which, I trust, shall witness live in brass of this day's work

Those that leave their valiant bones in France, dying like men, though buried in your dunghills, they shall be famed; for there the sun shall greet them, and draw their honours reeking up to heaven

Leaving their earthly parts to choke your clime, the smell whereof shall breed a plague in France.

Mark then abounding valour in our English, that being dead, like to the bullet's grazing, break out into a second course of mischief, killing in relapse of mortality.

Let me speak proudly

Tell the constable we are but warriors for the working-day

Our gayness and our gilt are all besmirched with rainy marching in the painful field

There's not a piece of feather in our host…

Good argument, I hope, we will not fly…

Time hath worn us into slovenry, but, by the mass, our hearts are in the trim

My poor soldiers tell me, yet ere night they'll be in fresher robes, or they will pluck the gay new coats over the French soldiers' heads and turn them out of service.

If they do this…

As, if God please, they shall…

My ransom then will soon be levied. Herald, save thou thy labour

Come thou no more for ransom, gentle herald, they shall have none, I swear, but these my joints

Which if they have as I will leave them, shall yield them little, tell the constable.

Montjoy

I shall, King Harry. And so fare thee well, thou never shalt hear herald any more.

(Exit)

King Henry 5

I fear though it once more come again for ransom.

(York enters)

York

My lord, most humbly on my knee I beg the leading of the forward.

King Henry 5

Take it, brave York. Now, soldiers, march away:

And how thou pleasest, God, dispose the day!

(Exit)

Act 4 Scene 4

The field of battle.

Alarum. Excursions.

(Pistol, French Soldier, and Boy enter)

Pistol

Yield, cur!

French Soldier

I think you are gentlemen of good quality

Pistol

Quality calame culture!

Art thou a gentleman?

What is thy name? Discuss.

French Soldier

Oh Seigneur Dieu!

Pistol

Oh, Signieur Dew should be a gentleman, perpend my words, oh Signieur Dew, and mark

Oh Signieur Dew, thou diest on point of fox, except, oh signieur, thou do give to me egregious ransom.

French Soldier

Oh, take mercy! Have pity on me!

Pistol

Moy shall not serve; I will have forty moys

Or I will fetch thy rim out at thy throat in drops of crimson blood.

French Soldier

Is it possible to escape the forces of your arms?

Pistol

Brass, cur!

Thou damned and luxurious mountain goat, offer'st me brass?

French Soldier

Oh parden me!

Pistol

Say'st thou me so? is that a ton of moys?

Come hither, boy, ask me this slave in French what is his name.

Boy

Listen, how are you named?

French Soldier

Monsieur le Fer.

Boy

He says his name is Master Fer.

Pistol

Master Fer! I'll fer him, and firk him, and ferret

Him, discuss the same in French unto him.

Boy

I do not know the French for fer, and ferret, and firk.

Pistol

Bid him to prepare, for I will cut his throat.

French Soldier

What says he, mister?

Boy

He commands me to inform you to be ready, for this solder here is disposed this hour to cut your throat

Pistol

Ow, cut throat, per my faith

Peasant, unless thou give me crowns, brave crowns

Mangled shalt thou be by this my sword.

French Soldier

Oh, I beg of you, by the love of God, forgive me!

I am a gentlemen of a good house, keep me alive, and I will give you 200 hundred crowns.

Pistol

What are his words?

Boy

He prays you to save his life

He is a gentleman of a good house

For his ransom he will give you two hundred crowns.

Pistol

Tell him my fury shall abate, and I the crowns will take.

French Soldier

Little mister, what says he?

Boy

Again, it is against his judgment to pardon any prisoner; nevertheless, for the crowns you have promised, he is glad to give you liberty, with honesty.

French Soldier

On my knees I give you a thousand thanks, and I esteem myself happy, I am fallen between the hands of a knight, most brave, valiant, and very distinguished noble of England

Pistol

Expound unto me, boy.

Boy

He gives you, upon his knees, a thousand thanks; and he esteems himself happy that he hath fallen into the hands of one, as he thinks, the most brave, valorous, and thrice-worthy signieur of England.

Pistol

As I suck blood, I will some mercy show.

Follow me!

Boy

Follow the great captain ?

(Pistol, and French Soldier exit)

I did never know so full a voice issue from so empty a heart, but the saying is true, the empty vessel makes the greatest sound.

Bardolph and Nym had ten times more valour than this roaring devil in the old play, that every one may pare his nails with a wooden dagger

They are both hanged

So would this be, if he durst steal any thing adventurously.

I must stay with the lackeys, with the luggage of our camp, the French might have a good prey of us, if he knew of it; for there is none to guard it but boys.

(Exits)

Act 4 Scene 5

Another part of the field.

(Constable, Orleans, Bourbon, Dauphin, and Rambures enter)

Constable

Oh diable!

Orleans

Oh lord! The day is lost, all is lost!

Dauphin

Death of my life! All is confounded, all!

Reproach and everlasting shame sits mocking in our plumes.

Oh merchante fortune!

Do not run away.

A short alarum

Constable

Why, all our ranks are broke.

Dauphin

Oh perdurable shame! let's stab ourselves.

Be these the wretches that we played at dice for?

Orleans

Is this the king we sent to for his ransom?

Bourbon

Shame and eternal shame, nothing but shame!

Let us die in honour, once more back again

He that will not follow Bourbon now, let him go hence, and with his cap in hand, like a base pander, hold the chamber-door whilst by a slave, no gentler than my dog, his fairest daughter is contaminated.

Constable

Disorder, that hath spoiled us, friend us now!

Let us on heaps go offer up our lives.

Orleans

We are now yet living in the field to smother up the English in our throngs, if any order might be thought upon.

Bourbon

The devil take order now! I'll to the throng, let life be short

Shame will be too long.

(Exits)

Act 4 Scene 6

Another part of the field.

Alarums.

(King Henry and forces, Exeter, and others enter)

King Henry 5

Well have we done, thrice valiant countrymen, but all's not done

Yet keep the French the field.

Exeter

The Duke of York commends him to your majesty.

King Henry 5

Lives he, good uncle? thrice within this hour I saw him down; thrice up again and fighting

From helmet to the spur all blood he was.

Exeter

In which array, brave soldier, doth he lie, larding the plain; and by his bloody side, yoke-fellow to his honour-owing wounds, the noble Earl of Suffolk also lies.

Suffolk first died: and York, all haggled over, comes to him, where in gore he lay instepped, and takes him by the beard; kisses the gashes that bloodily did spawn upon his face

And cries aloud 'Tarry, dear cousin Suffolk!

My soul shall thine keep company to heaven

Tarry, sweet soul, for mine, then fly abreast, as in this glorious and well-foughten field we kept together in our chivalry!

Upon these words I came and cheered him up, he smiled me in the face, taught me his hand, and with a feeble gripe says dear my lord, commend my service to me sovereign.

So did he turn and over Suffolk's neck he threw his wounded arm and kiss'd his lips

So espoused to death, with blood he sealed a testament of noble-ending love.

The pretty and sweet manner of it forced those waters from me which I would have stopped

I had not so much of man in me, and all my mother came into mine eyes and gave me up to tears.

King Henry 5

I blame you not

For, hearing this, I must perforce compound with mistful eyes, or they will issue too.

(Alarum)

But, hark! what new alarum is this same?

The French have reinforced their scattered men, then every soldier kill his prisoners, give the word through. **(Exit)**

Act 4 Scene 7

Another part of the field.

(Fluellen and Gower enter)

Fluellen

Kill the poys and the luggage! It is expressly against the law of arms, it is as arrant a piece of knavery, mark you now, as can be offer it

In your conscience, now, is it not?

Gower

It is certain there's not a boy left alive

The cowardly rascals that ran from the battle hall done this slaughter: besides, they have burned and carried away all that was in the king's tent

Wherefore the king, most worthily, hath caused every soldier to cut his prisoner's throat.

Oh, it is a gallant king!

Fluellen

Ay, he was porn at Monmouth, Captain Gower.

What call you the town's name where Alexander the Pig was born!

Gower

Alexander the Great.

Fluellen

Why, I pray you, is not pig great? The pig, or the

great, or the mighty, or the huge, or the magnanimous, are all one reckonings, save the phrase is a little variations.

Gower

I think Alexander the Great was born in Macedon

His father was called Philip of Macedon, as I take it.

Fluellen

I think it is in Macedon where Alexander is porn.

I tell you, captain, if you look in the maps of the world, I warrant you all, find in the comparisons between Macedon and Monmouth that the situations look you, is both alike. There is a river in Macedon

There is also moreover a river at Monmouth: it is called Wye at Monmouth; but it is out of my prains what is the name of the other river

It is all one, it is alike as my fingers is to my fingers, and there is salmons in both.

If you mark Alexander's life well, Harry of Monmouth's life is come after it indifferent well

For there is figures in all things.

Alexander, God knows, and you know, in his rages, and his furies, and his wraths, and his cholers, and his moods, and his displeasures, and his indignations, and also being a little intoxicates in his prains, did, in his ales and his angers, look you, kill his best friend, Cleitus.

Gower

Our king is not like him in that: he never killed any of his friends.

Fluellen

It is not well done, mark you now take the tales out of my mouth, ere it is made and finished.

I speak but in the figures and comparisons of it, as Alexander killed his friend Cleitus, being in his ales and his cups

Also Harry Monmouth, being in his right wits and his good judgments, turned away the fat knight with the great belly-doublet, he was full of jests, and gipes, and knaveries, and mocks

I have forgot his name.

Gower

Sir John Falstaff.

Fluellen

That is he: I'll tell you there is good men porn at Monmouth.

Gower

Here comes his majesty.

(Alarum)

(King Henry, and forces; Warwick, Gloucester, Exeter, and others enter)

King Henry 5

I was not angry since I came to France until this instant. Take a trumpet, herald

Ride thou unto the horsemen on yon hill, if they will fight with us, bid them come down, or void the field

They do offend our sight, if they'll do neither, we will come to them and make them skirr away, as swift as stones enforced from the old Assyrian slings

Besides, we'll cut the throats of those we have, and not a man of them that we shall take shall taste our mercy.

Go and tell them so.

(Montjoy enter)

Exeter

Here comes the herald of the French, my liege.

Gloucester

His eyes are humbler than they used to be.

King Henry 5

How now! what means this, herald? know'st thou not that I have fined these bones of mine for ransom?

Comest thou again for ransom?

Montjoy

No, great king, I come to thee for charitable license, that we may wander over this bloody field to look our dead, and then to bury them

To sort our nobles from our common men. for many of our princes-- woe the while!...

Lie drowned and soaked in mercenary blood

So do our vulgar drench their peasant limbs in blood of princes; and their wounded steeds fret fetlock deep in gore and with wild rage yerk out their armed heels at their dead masters, killing them twice.

Oh give us leave, great king, to view the field in safety and dispose of their dead bodies!

King Henry 5

I tell thee truly, herald, I know not if the day be ours or no

For yet a many of your horsemen peer and gallop over the field.

Montjoy

The day is yours.

King Henry 5

Praised be God, and not our strength, for it!

What is this castle called that stands hard by?

Montjoy

They call it Agincourt.

King Henry 5

Then call we this the field of Agincourt, fought on the day of Crispin Crispianus.

Fluellen

Your grandfather of famous memory, another please your majesty, and your great-uncle Edward the Black, Prince of Wales, as I have read in the chronicles, fought a most brave battle here in France.

King Henry 5

They did, Fluellen.

Fluellen

Your majesty says very true: if your majesties is remembered of it, the Welshmen did good service in a garden where leeks did grow, wearing leeks in their Monmouth caps

Your majesty know, to this hour is an honourable badge of the service

I do believe your majesty takes no scorn to wear the leek upon Saint Tavy's day.

King Henry 5

I wear it for a memorable honour

For I am Welsh, you know, good countryman.

Fluellen

All the water in Wye cannot wash your majesty's Welsh plood out of your pody, I can tell you that, God bless it and preserve it, as long as it pleases his grace, and his majesty too!

King Henry 5

Thanks, good my countryman.

Fluellen

By Jesus, I am your majesty's countryman, I care not who know it

I will confess it to all the world, I need not to be ashamed of your majesty, praised be God, so long as your majesty is an honest man.

King Henry 5

God keep me so! Our heralds go with him, bring me just notice of the numbers dead on both our parts.

Call yonder fellow hither

(Points to William)

(Heralds exits with Montjoy)

Exeter

Soldier, you must come to the king.

King Henry 5

Soldier, why wearest thou that glove in thy cap?

Williams

Another please your majesty, it is the gage of one that I should fight withal, if he be alive.

King Henry 5

An Englishman?

Williams

Another please your majesty, a rascal that swaggered with me last night.

Who, if alive and ever dare to challenge this glove, I have sworn to take him a box on the ear

If I can see my glove in his cap, which he swore, as he was a soldier, he would wear if alive, I will strike it out soundly.

King Henry 5

What think you, Captain Fluellen? is it fit this soldier keep his oath?

Fluellen

He is a craven and a villain else, another please your majesty, in my conscience.

King Henry 5

It may be his enemy is a gentleman of great sort, quite from the answer of his degree.

Fluellen

Though he be as good a gentleman as the devil is, as Lucifer and Belzebub himself, it is necessary, look your grace, that he keep his vow and his oath.

If he be perjured, see you now, his reputation is as arrant a villain and a Jacksauce, as ever his black shoe trod upon God's ground and his earth, in my conscience, la!

King Henry 5

Then keep thy vow, sirrah, when thou meetest the fellow.

Williams

So I will, my liege, as I live.

King Henry 5

Who servest thou under?

Williams

Under Captain Gower, my liege.

Fluellen

Gower is a good captain, and is good knowledge and literatured in the wars.

King Henry 5

Call him hither to me, soldier.

Williams

I will, my liege.

(Exit)

King Henry 5

Here, Fluellen; wear thou this favour for me and stick it in thy cap, when Alencon and myself were down together, I plucked this glove from his helm, if any man challenge this, he is a friend to Alencon, and an enemy to our person

If thou encounter any such, apprehend him, an thou dost me love.

Fluellen

Your grace doo's me as great honours as can be desired in the hearts of his subjects, I would fain see the man, that has but two legs, that shall find himself aggrieved at this glove; that is all

I would fain see it once, an please God of his grace that I might see.

King Henry 5

Knowest thou Gower?

Fluellen

He is my dear friend, an please you.

King Henry 5

Pray thee, go seek him, and bring him to my tent.

Fluellen

I will fetch him.

(Exit)

King Henry 5

My Lord of Warwick, and my brother Gloucester, follow Fluellen closely at the heels, the glove which I have given him for a favour may haply purchase him a box on the ear

It is the soldier's

By bargain should wear it myself.

Follow, good cousin Warwick, if that the soldier strike him, as I judge by his blunt bearing he will keep his word, some sudden mischief may arise of it

For I do know Fluellen valiant and touched with choler, hot as gunpowder, and quickly will return an injury, follow and see there be no harm between them.

Go you with me, uncle of Exeter.

(Exit)

Act 4 Scene 8

Before King Henry'S pavilion.

(Gower and Williams enter)

Williams

I warrant it is to knight you, captain.

(Fluellen enter)

Fluellen

God's will and his pleasure, captain, I beseech you now, come apace to the king, there is more good toward you peradventure than is in your knowledge to dream of.

Williams

Sir, know you this glove?

Fluellen

Know the glove! I know the glove is glove.

Williams

I know this; and thus I challenge it.

(Strikes him)

Fluellen

Is Blood, an arrant traitor as any is in the universal world, or in France, or in England!

Gower

How now, sir! you villain!

Williams

Do you think I'll be forsworn?

Fluellen

Stand away, Captain Gower; I will give treason his payment into ploughs, I warrant you.

Williams

I am no traitor.

Fluellen

That's a lie in thy throat. I charge you in his majesty's name, apprehend him, he's a friend of the Duke Alencon's.

(Warwick and Gloucester enter)

Warwick

How now, how now! what's the matter?

Fluellen

My Lord of Warwick, here is--praised be God for it!...

A most contagious treason come to light, look you, as you shall desire in a summer's day.

Here is his majesty.

(King Henry and Exeter enter)

King Henry 5

How now! what's the matter?

Fluellen

My liege, here is a villain and a traitor, that, look your grace, has struck the glove which your majesty is take out of the helmet of Alencon.

Williams

My liege, this was my glove; here is the fellow of it

He that I gave it to in change promised to wear it in his cap. I promised to strike him, if he did

I met this man with my glove in his cap, and I have been as good as my word.

Fluellen

Your majesty hear now, saving your majesty's manhood, what an arrant, rascally, beggarly, lousy knave it is

I hope your majesty is pear me testimony and witness, and will avouchment, that this is the glove of Alencon, that your majesty is give me; in your conscience, now?

King Henry 5

Give me thy glove, soldier: look, here is the fellow of it.

It was I, indeed, thou promised'st to strike

Thou hast given me most bitter terms.

Fluellen

An please your majesty, let his neck answer for it, if there is any martial law in the world.

King Henry 5

How canst thou make me satisfaction?

Williams

All offences, my lord, come from the heart: never came any from mine that might offend your majesty.

King Henry 5

It was ourself thou didst abuse.

Williams

Your majesty came not like yourself: you appeared to me but as a common man.

Witness the night, your garments, your lowliness; and what your highness suffered under that shape, I beseech you take it for your own fault and not mine, for had you been as I took you for, I made no offence

Therefore, I beseech your highness, pardon me.

King Henry 5

Here, uncle Exeter, fill this glove with crowns, and give it to this fellow.

Keep it, fellow

And wear it for an honour in thy cap till I do challenge it.

Give him the crowns, and captain, you must needs be friends with him.

Fluellen

By this day and this light, the fellow has mettle enough in his belly.

Hold, there is twelve pence for you

I pray you to serve Got, and keep you out of prawls, and prabbles' and quarrels, and dissensions, and, I warrant you, it is the better for you.

Williams

I will none of your money.

Fluellen

It is with a good will

I can tell you, it will serve you to mend your shoes: come, wherefore should you be so bashful?

Your shoes is not so good, it is a good selling, I warrant you, or I will change it.

(An English Herald enter)

King Henry 5

Now, herald, are the dead numbered?

Herald

Here is the number of the slaughtered French.

King Henry 5

What prisoners of good sort are taken, uncle?

Exeter

Charles Duke of Orleans, nephew to the king

John Duke of Bourbon, and Lord Bouciqualt, of other lords and barons, knights and squires, full fifteen hundred, besides common men.

King Henry 5

This note doth tell me of ten thousand French that in the field lie slain, of princes, in this number, and nobles bearing banners, there lie dead one hundred twenty six

Added to these, of knights, esquires, and gallant gentlemen, eight thousand and four hundred

Of the which, Five hundred were but yesterday dubbed knights, so that in these ten thousand they have lost, there are but sixteen hundred mercenaries

The rest are princes, barons, lords, knights, squires, and gentlemen of blood and quality.

The names of those their nobles that lie dead, Charles Delabreth, high constable of France

Jaques of Chatillon, admiral of France

The master of the cross-bows, Lord Rambures

Great Master of France, the brave Sir Guichard Dolphin, John Duke of Alencon, Anthony Duke of Brabant, the brother of the Duke of Burgundy, and Edward Duke of Bar: of lusty earls, Grandpre and Roussi, Fauconberg and Foix, Beaumont and Marle, Vaudemont and Lestrale.

Here was a royal fellowship of death!

Where is the number of our Englis dead?

Herald shews him another paper Edward the Duke of York, the Earl of Suffolk, sir Richard Ketly, Davy Gam, esquire

None else of name

Of all other men, but five and twenty.

Oh God, thy arm was here

And not to us, but to thy arm alone, ascribe we all!

When, without stratagem, but in plain shock and even play of battle, was ever known so great and little loss on one part and on the other?

Take it, God,

For it is none but thine!

Exeter

It is wonderful!

King Henry 5

Come, go we in procession to the village.

And be it death proclaimed through our host to boast of this or take the praise from God which is his only.

Fluellen

Is it not lawful, an please your majesty, to tell how many is killed?

King Henry 5

Yes, captain; but with this acknowledgement, that God fought for us.

Fluellen

Yes, my conscience, he did us great good.

King Henry 5

Do we all holy rites;

Let there be sung 'Non nobis' and 'Te Deum;'

The dead with charity enclosed in clay, and then to Calais

To England then, where ne'er from France arrived more happy men.

(Exit)

Act 5 Intro

(Chorus enters)

Chorus

Vouchsafe to those that have not read the story, that I may prompt them, and of such as have, I humbly pray them to admit the excuse of time, of numbers and due course of things, which cannot in their huge and proper life be here presented.

Now we bear the king Toward Calais, grant him there

There seen, heave him away upon your winged thoughts athwart the sea.

Behold, the English beach Pales in the flood with men, with wives and boys, whose shouts and claps out-voice the deep mouthed sea, which like a mighty whiffler before the king seems to prepare his way: so let him land, and solemnly see him set on to London.

So swift a pace hath thought that even now you may imagine him upon Blackheath

Where that his lords desire him to have borne his bruised helmet and his bended sword before him through the city, he forbids it, being free from vainness and self-glorious pride

Giving full trophy, signal and ostent quite from himself to God.

But now behold, in the quick forge and working-house of thought, how London doth pour out her citizens!

The mayor and all his brethren in best sort,

Like to the senators of the antique Rome, with the plebeians swarming at their heels, go forth and fetch their conquering Caesar in

As, by a lower but loving likelihood, were now the general of our gracious empress, as in good time he may, from Ireland coming

Bringing rebellion broached on his sword, how many would the peaceful city quit, to welcome him! much more, and much more cause, did they this Harry. Now in London place him

As yet the lamentation of the French invites the King of England's stay at home

The emperor's coming in behalf of France, to order peace between them; and omit all the occurrences, whatever chanced, till Harry's back-return again to France

There must we bring him; and myself have played

The interim, by remembering you it is past.

Then brook abridgment, and your eyes advance, after your thoughts, straight back again to France.

(Exits)

Act 5 Scene 1

France. The Englis camp.

(Fluellen and Gower enter)

Gower

Nay, that's right; but why wear you your leek today?

Saint Davy's day is past.

Fluellen

There is occasions and causes why and wherefore in all things, I will tell you, ask my friend, Captain Gower: the rascally, scald, beggarly, lousy, bragging knave, Pistol, which you and yourself and all the world know to be no better than a fellow

Look you now, of no merits, he is come to me and brings me bread and salt yesterday, look you, and bid me eat my leek, it was in place where I could not breed no contention with him

I will be so bold as to wear it in my cap till I see him once again, and then I will tell him a little piece of my desires.

(Pistol enters)

Gower

Why, here he comes, swelling like a turkey-cock.

Fluellen

It is no matter for his swellings nor his turkey-cocks.

God bless you, Aunchient Pistol!

You scurvy, lousy knave, God bless you!

Pistol

Ha! art thou bedlam? dost thou thirst, base Trojan, to have me fold up Parca's fatal web?

Hence! I am qualmis at the smell of leek.

Fluellen

I beseech you heartily, scurvy, lousy knave, at my desires, and my requests, and my petitions, to eat, look you, this leek

Look you, you do not love it, nor your affections and your appetites and your digestions doo's not agree with it, I would desire you to eat it.

Pistol

Not for Cadwallader and all his goats.

Fluellen

There is one goat for you.

(Strikes him)

Will you be so good, scauld knave, as eat it?

Pistol

Base Trojan, thou shalt die.

Fluellen

You say very true, scauld knave, when God's will is, I will desire you to live in the mean time, and eat your victuals

Come, there is sauce for it.

(Strikes him)

You called me yesterday mountain-squire

I will make you to-day a squire of low degree. I pray you, fall to, if you can mock a leek, you can eat a leek.

Gower

Enough, captain: you have astonished him.

Fluellen

I say, I will make him eat some part of my leek, or

I will peat his pate four days.

Bite, I pray you

It is good for your green wound and your bloody coxcomb.

Pistol

Must I bite?

Fluellen

Yes, certainly, and out of doubt and out of question too, and ambiguities.

Pistol

By this leek, I will most horribly revenge, I eat and eat, I swear…

Fluellen

Eat, I pray you: will you have some more sauce to your leek? There is not enough leek to swear by.

Pistol

Quiet thy cudgel; thou dost see I eat.

Fluellen

Much good do you, scauld knave, heartily.

Nay, pray you, throw none away

The skin is good for your broken coxcomb.

When you take occasions to see leeks hereafter, I pray you, mock at them; that is all.

Pistol

Good.

Fluellen

Ay, leeks is good: hold you, there is a groat to heal your pate.

Pistol

Me a groat!

Fluellen

Yes, verily and in truth, you shall take it

I have another leek in my pocket, which you shall eat.

Pistol

I take thy groat in earnest of revenge.

Fluellen

If I owe you any thing, I will pay you in cudgels, you shall be a woodmonger, and buy nothing of me but cudgels.

God be win you, and keep you, and heal your pate.

(Exit)

Pistol

All hell shall stir for this.

Gower

Go, go

You are a counterfeit cowardly knave.

Will you mock at an ancient tradition, begun upon an honourable respect, and worn as a memorable trophy of predeceased valour and dare not avouch in your deeds any of your words?

I have seen you gleeking and galling at this gentleman twice or thrice.

You thought, because he could not speak English in the native garb, he could not therefore handle an English cudgel, you find it otherwise

Henceforth let a Welsh correction teach you a good English condition. Fare ye well.

(Exit)

Pistol

Doth Fortune play the huswife with me now?

News have I, that my Nell is dead in the spital of malady of France

There, my rendezvous is quite cut off.

Old I do wax; and from my weary limbs honour is cudgelled.

Well, bawd I'll turn, and something lean to cutpurse of quick hand.

To England will I steal, and there I'll steal, and patches will I get unto these cudgell'd scars, and swear I got them in the Gallia wars.

(Exit)

Act 5 Scene 2

France. A royal palace.

(Enter: At one door King Henry, Exeter, Bedford, Gloucester, Warwick, Westmoreland, and other Lords; at another, the French King, Queen Isabel, the Princess Katharine, Alice and other Ladies; the Duke of Burgundy, and his train)

King Henry 5

Peace to this meeting, wherefore we are met!

Unto our brother France, and to our sister, health and fair time of day; joy and good wishes to our most fair and princely cousin Katharine

As a branch and member of this royalty, by whom this great assembly is contrived, we do salute you, Duke of Burgundy

Princes French, and peers, health to you all!

King of France

Right joyous are we to behold your face, most worthy brother England

Fairly met, so are you, princes English, every one.

Queen Isabel

So happy be the issue, brother England, of this good day and of this gracious meeting, as we are now glad to behold your eyes

Your eyes, which hitherto have borne in them against the French, that met them in their bent, the fatal balls of murdering basilisks, the venom of such looks, we fairly hope have lost their quality, and that this day shall change all griefs and quarrels into love.

King Henry 5

To cry amen to that, thus we appear.

Queen Isabel

You English princes all, I do salute you.

Burgundy

My duty to you both, on equal love, great Kings of France and England! That I have labour'd, with all my wits, my pains and strong endeavours, to bring your most imperial majesties unto this bar and royal interview.

Your mightiness on both parts best can witness.

Since then my office hath so far prevailed that, face to face and royal eye to eye, you have congreeted, let it not disgrace me

If I demand, before this royal view, what rub or what impediment there is, why that the naked, poor and mangled Peace, dear nurse of arts and joyful births should not in this best garden of the world our fertile France, put up her lovely visage?

Alas, she hath from France too long been chased, and all her husbandry doth lie on heaps, corrupting in its own fertility.

Her vine, the merry cheerer of the heart, unpruned dies

Her hedges even-pleached, like prisoners wildly overgrown with hair, put forth disordered twigs

Her fallow leas the darnel, hemlock and rank fumitory doth root upon, while that the coulter rusts that should deracinate such savagery

The even mead, that worst brought sweetly forth the freckled cowslip, burnet and green clover, wanting the scythe, all uncorrected, rank, conceives by idleness and nothing teems, but hateful docks, rough thistles, kecksies, blurs, losing both beauty and utility.

And as our vineyards, fallows, meads and hedges, defective in their natures, grow to wildness, even so our houses and ourselves and children have lost, or do not learn for want of time, the sciences that should become our country

Grow like savages…

As soldiers will that nothing do but meditate on blood…

To swearing and stern looks, diffused attire and every thing that seems unnatural.

Which to reduce into our former favour you are assembled

My speech entreats that I may know the let, why gentle Peace should not expel these inconveniences and bless us with her former qualities.

King Henry 5

If, Duke of Burgundy, you would the peace, whose want gives growth to the imperfections which you have cited, you must buy that peace with full accord to all our just demands

Whose tenors and particular effects you have enscheduled briefly in your hands.

Burgundy

The king hath heard them; to the which as yet there is no answer made.

King Henry 5

Well then the peace, which you before so urged, lies in his answer.

King of France

I have but with a cursorary eye overglanced the articles, pleaseth your grace to appoint some of your council presently to sit with us once more, with better heed to re-survey them, we will suddenly pass our accept and peremptory answer.

King Henry 5

Brother, we shall. Go, uncle Exeter, and brother Clarence, and you, brother Gloucester, Warwick and Huntingdon, go with the king

Take with you free power to ratify, augment, or alter, as your wisdoms best shall see advantageable for our dignity, anything in or out of our demands, and we'll consign thereto.

Will you, fair sister, go with the princes, or stay here with us?

Queen Isabel

Our gracious brother, I will go with them, haply a woman's voice may do some good, when articles too nicely urged be stood on.

King Henry 5

Yet leave our cousin Katharine here with us, she is our capital demand, comprised within the fore-rank of our articles.

Queen Isabel

She hath good leave.

(All exit except Henry, Katharine, and Alice)

King Henry 5

Fair Katharine, and most fair, will you vouchsafe to teach a soldier terms such as will enter at a lady's ear and plead his love-suit to her gentle heart?

Katharine

Your majesty shall mock at me; I cannot speak your England.

King Henry 5

Oh fair Katharine, if you will love me soundly with your French heart, I will be glad to hear you confess it brokenly with your Englis tongue.

Do you like me, Kate?

Katharine

Parden me, I cannot tell what is like me.

King Henry 5

An angel is like you, Kate, and you are like an angel.

Katharine

What says he? I am similar to an Angel?

Alice

Yes, verily, except your grace, indeed says he.

King Henry 5

I said so, dear Katharine; and I must not blush to affirm it.

Katharine

Oh good God! The langages of men are full of trophies.

King Henry 5

What says she, fair one? that the tongues of men are full of deceits?

Alice

Yes, that the tongues of men are full of deceit, that is the princess

King Henry 5

The princess is the better Englishwoman.

In faith, Kate, my wooing is fit for thy understanding, I am glad thou canst speak no better English

For, if thou couldst, thou wouldst find me such a plain king that thou wouldst think I had sold my farm to buy my crown.

I know no ways to mince it in love, but directly to say I love you, then if you urge me farther than to say do you in faith?

I wear out my suit.

Give me your answer

In faith, do, and so clap hands and a bargain, how say you, lady?

Katharine

Save your honour, me understand well

King Henry 5

Marry, if you would put me to verses or to dance for your sake, Kate, why you undid me

For the one, I have neither words nor measure, and for the other, I have no strength in measure, yet a reasonable measure in strength.

If I could win a lady at leap-frog, or by vaulting into my saddle with my armour on my back, under the correction of bragging be it spoken.

I should quickly leap into a wife, or if I might buffet for my love, or bound my horse for her favours, I could lay on like a butcher and sit like a jack-an-apes, never off.

But, before God, Kate, I cannot look greenly nor gasp out my eloquence, nor I have no cunning in protestation

Only downright oaths, which I never use till urged, nor never break for urging.

If thou canst love a fellow of this temper, Kate, whose face is not worth sun-burning, that never looks in his glass for love of anything he sees there, let thine eye be thy cook.

I speak to thee plain soldier, if thou canst love me for this, take me, if not, to say to thee that I shall die, is true

For thy love, by the Lord, no

I love thee too.

And while thou livest, dear Kate, take a fellow of plain and uncoined constancy

For he perforce must do thee right, because he hath not the gift to woo in other places

These fellows of infinite tongue, that can rhyme themselves into ladies' favours, they do always reason themselves out again.

What! A speaker is but a prater; a rhyme is but a ballad.

A good leg will fall; a straight back will stoop

A black beard will turn white; a curled pate will grow

Bald

A fair face will wither

A full eye will wax hollow: but a good heart, Kate, is the sun and the moon

Rather, the sun, and not the moon

For it shines bright and never changes, but keeps his course truly.

If thou would have such a one, take me

Take me, take a soldier; take a soldier, take a king.

What sayest thou then to my love?

Speak, my fair, and fairly, I pray thee.

Katharine

Is it possible dat I sould love de enemy of France?

King Henry 5

No

It is not possible you should love the enemy of France, Kate, but, in loving me, you should love the friend of France

For I love France so well that I will not part with a village of it

I will have it all mine, and, Kate, when France is mine and I am yours, then yours is France and you are mine.

Katharine

I cannot tell vat is dat.

King Henry 5

No, Kate? I will tell thee in French

Which I am sure will hang upon my tongue like a new-married wife about her husband's neck, hardly to be shook off.

I am now upon the possession of France and when you have possession of me, what then?

Saint Denis be my speed!... Hence yours is France and you are mine.

It is as easy for me, Kate, to conquer the kingdom as to speak so much more French, I shall never move thee in French, unless it be to laugh at me.

Katharine

Save your honor, the French you speak, is better than the English I speak

King Henry 5

No, have faith, is it not, Kate, but thy speaking of my tongue, and I thine

Most truly-falsely, most needs be granted to be much at one.

But, Kate, dost thou understand thus much English, canst thou love me?

Katharine

I cannot tell.

King Henry 5

Can any of your neighbours tell, Kate?

I'll ask them.

Come, I know thou lovest me: and at night, when you come into your closet, you'll question this gentlewoman about me

I know, Kate, you will to her dispraise those parts in me that you love with your heart, but good Kate, mock me mercifully

The rather, gentle princess, because I love thee cruelly.

If ever thou best mine, Kate, as I have a saving faith within me tells me thou shalt, I get thee with scambling, and thou must therefore needs prove a good soldier-breeder: shall not thou and I, between Saint Denis and Saint George, compound a boy, half French, half English, that shall go to Constantinople and take the Turk by the beard?

Shall we not? what sayest thou, my fair flower-de-luce?

Katharine

I do not know that

King Henry 5

No

It is hereafter to know, but now to promise, do but now promise, Kate, you will endeavour for your French part of such a boy

For my Englis moiety take the word of a king and a bachelor.

How answer you, la plus belle Katharine du monde, mon tres cher et devin deesse?

Katharine

Your majesty with false French enough to deceive the most sage demoiselle that is en France.

King Henry 5

Now, fie upon my false French!

By mine honour, in true English, I love thee, Kate, by which honour I dare not swear thou lovest me

Yet my blood begins to flatter me that thou dost, notwithstanding the poor and untempering effect of my visage.

Now, beshrew my father's ambition!

He was thinking of civil wars when he got me: therefore was I created with a stubborn outside, with an aspect of iron, that, when I come to woo ladies, I fright them.

In faith, Kate, the elder I wax, the better I shall appear, my comfort is, that old age, that ill layer up of beauty, can do no more, spoil upon my face, thou hast me, if thou hast me, at the worst

Thou shalt wear me, if thou wear me, better and better,

and therefore tell me, most fair Katharine, will you

have me?

Put off your maiden blushes; avouch the thoughts of your heart with the looks of an empress

Take me by the hand, and say Harry of England I am

Thine, which word thou shalt no sooner bless mine ear withal, but I will tell thee aloud England is thine, Ireland is thine, France is thine, and Harry Plantagenet is thine

Though I speak it before his face, if he be not fellow with the best king, thou shalt find the best king of good fellows.

Come, your answer in broken music; for thy voice is music and thy Englis broken

Queen of all, Katharine, break thy mind to me in broken English

Wilt thou have me?

Katharine

That is as it is all please the king my father.

King Henry 5

Nay, it will please him well, Kate it shall please him, Kate.

Katharine

Than it is all also content to me

King Henry 5

Upon that I kiss your hand, and I call you my queen.

Katharine

Leave, my noble, leave, leave

My faith, I do not want to lower your grandeur by lowering the hand of your lordship as an unworthy servant

Excuse me, I beg of you, my most powerful noble

King Henry 5

Then I will kiss your lips, Kate.

Katharine

Dames and ladies to be deflowered before their wedding, it is not the custom of France.

King Henry 5

Madam my interpreter, what says she?

Alice

That it is not be de fashion pour les ladies of

France…

I cannot tell you what deflowering means.

King Henry 5

Say then, instead, to kiss.

Alice

Your majesty has heard better than I

King Henry 5

It is not a fashion for the maids in France to kiss before they are married, would she say?

Alice

Yes, really.

King Henry 5

Oh Kate, nice customs curtsy to great kings.

Dear Kate, you and I cannot be confined within the weak list of a country's fashion, we are the makers of manners, Kate

The liberty that follows our places stops the mouth of all find-faults

As I will do yours, for upholding the nice fashion of your country in denying me a kiss, therefore, patiently and yielding

(Kisses her)

You have witchcraft in your lips, Kate, there is more eloquence in a sugar touch of them than in the tongues of the French council

They should sooner persuade Harry of England than a general petition of monarchs.

Here comes your father.

(The French King and his Queen re-enter, then, Burgundy, and other Lords)

Burgundy

God save your majesty!

My royal cousin, teach you our princess English?

King Henry 5

I would have her learn, my fair cousin, how perfectly I love her

That is good English.

Burgundy

Is she not apt?

King Henry 5

Our tongue is rough, coz, and my condition is not smooth

Having neither the voice nor the heart of flattery about me, I cannot so conjure up the spirit of love in her, that he will appear in his true likeness.

Burgundy

Pardon the frankness of my mirth, if I answer you for that.

If you would conjure in her, you must make a circle

If conjure up love in her in his true likeness, he must appear naked and blind.

Can you blame her then, being a maid yet rosed over with the virgin crimson of modesty, if she deny the appearance of a naked blind boy in her naked seeing self?

It were, my lord, a hard condition for a maid to consign to.

King Henry 5

Yet they do wink and yield, as love is blind and enforces.

Burgundy

They are then excused, my lord, when they see not what they do.

King Henry 5

Then, good my lord, teach your cousin to consent winking.

Burgundy

I will wink on her to consent, my lord, if you will teach her to know my meaning, for maids, well summered and warm kept, are like flies at Bartholomew-tide, blind, though they have their eyes

Then they will endure handling, which before would not abide looking on.

King Henry 5

This moral ties me over to time and a hot summer

So I shall catch the fly, your cousin, in the latter end and she must be blind too.

Burgundy

As love is, my lord, before it loves.

King Henry 5

It is so, and you may, some of you, thank love for my blindness, who cannot see many a fair French city for one fair French maid that stands in my way.

French King

Yes, my lord, you see them prospectively, the cities turned into a maid

For they are all girdled with maiden walls that war hath never entered.

King Henry 5

Shall Kate be my wife?

French King

So please you.

King Henry 5

I am content

So the maiden cities you talk of may wait on her, so the maid that stood in the way for my wish shall show me the way to my will.

French King

We have consented to all terms of reason.

King Henry 5

Is it so, my lords of England?

Westmoreland

The king hath granted every article, his daughter first, and then in sequel all, according to their firm proposed natures.

Exeter

Only he hath not yet subscribed this, where your majesty demands, that the King of France, having any occasion to write for matter of grant, shall name your highness in this form and with this addition in French, our cheated son Henry King of England, inheritor of France

Thus in Latin: Praeclarissimus filius noster Henricus, Rex Angliae, et Haeres Franciae.

French King

Nor this I have not, brother, so denied, but your request shall make me let it pass.

King Henry 5

I pray you then, in love and dear alliance, let that one article rank with the rest

And thereupon give me your daughter.

French King

Take her, fair son, and from her blood raise up issue to me

That the contending kingdoms of France and England, whose very shores look pale with envy of each other's happiness may cease their hatred, and this dear conjunction plant neighbourhood and Christian-like accord in their sweet bosoms, that never war advance his bleeding sword 'twixt England and fair France.

ALL

Amen!

King Henry 5

Now, welcome, Kate

Bear me witness all, that here I kiss her as my sovereign queen.

(Flourish)

Queen Isabel

God, the best maker of all marriages, combine your hearts in one, your realms in one!

As man and wife, being two, are one in love, so be there between your kingdoms such a spousal, that never may ill office, or fell jealousy, which troubles often the bed of blessed marriage

Thrust in between the paction of these kingdoms, to make divorce of their incorporate league

That English may as French, French Englishmen, receive each other. God speak this Amen!

ALL

Amen!

King Henry 5

Prepare we for our marriage…

On which day, my Lord of Burgundy, we'll take your oath, and all the peers, for surety of our leagues.

Then shall I swear to Kate, and you to me

May our oaths well kept and prosperous be!

(Sennet)

(Exit)

Finally

(Chorus enters)

Chorus

Thus far, with rough and all-unable pen, our bending author hath pursued the story, in little room confining mighty men, mangling by starts the full course of their glory.

Small time, but in that small most greatly lived this star of England: Fortune made his sword

By which the world's best garden be achieved, and of it left his son imperial lord.

Henry the Sixth, in infant bands crowned King of France and England, did this king succeed

Whose state so many had the managing, that they lost France and made his England bleed, which often our stage hath shown

For their sake, in your fair minds let this acceptance take.

(Exit)

The End

Description of Titles

The Comedy of Errors
Caught in a land of embittered woman and war, caught in months of strife, where a merchant's visit offers little natural relief. The fleeting moment of approving gold, inspire further bitterness, upon an approach to the marketplace, and then the women that occupy within them. **19 Characters**

The Taming of the Shrew
Arrangements are made to spencer would be suiters to melt the splendors of a strong willed women. The winning is found pledged, influencing maids to seek their turns, and meanwhile terms required, an authentic spirit that they will/would wed soon. **34 Characters**

Love's Labor's Lost
The house of a scholarly pursuit, returns into an expressive, either poetic or drunken as highlighting the gold-slur filled house of charms and dance like rhymes **19 Characters**

A Midsummer Night's Dream
Journey into a land of fairies, where creatures are found to have the same issues as nobilities. Exemplifying, perhaps, there's no place like home. Meet fairies as they frolic and play the noble hearts and sway, posed in the recesses of night, and mystic lands of a faraway kingdom. **22 Characters**

The Merchant of Venice

An angry Shylock brings to trial a merchant, over a lover's quarrel disrupted, demanding pounds of flesh. With no desires for even three times the amount, the Shylock demands his vengeance at heart.   **22 Characters**

The Merry Wives of Windsor
Mistresses and lords try and relate towards one another, as various important community figures come to have their word/seek the hostesses. Pleasantries are exchanged as a range of charms are expressed, until conversation resembled so to folly.   **23 Characters**

Much Ado About Nothing
Soldiery level consideration occupy the gossip, as several hostilities are summoned up, onto heart related matter. Also in conflict. The latter portion of the story lightens up to a women's home and pleasantries. Thereafter, a general search and care in actions, creating response phrasing poetic to the responses of leadership parading, until an end full of sensitivity asking gently questions, onto kisses

23 Characters

As You Like It
Troubled lower nobles venture about daily business, with some mild graces towards the ladies found. In need of relief or play, the Duke and family members take to the woods, where jests of drinking turn into troubled amusements, or warmth of a women's heart.   **26 Characters**

Troilus and Cressida

The infamous Greek battle for Troy. A large army arrives to take back the lost love of a humiliated foe. Both sides mobilize heroes onto the field, as soldiers and generals move to the side, and let strategies and fate take their course.

21+ Characters

All's Well That Ends Well

A tale of delightful, womanly gossip of a prestigious sort, until the French King has his word on the excellence of others. The story initially revolves around a strong willed countess, whose courteous pose and insight, reflect a nobility reflective of the house and court (council). Dialogue therein revolving around the councils rather, to exemplify (court counselling women). **25 Characters**

Measure for Measure

Statesmen discourse leading with time to a personal reflection. Strolling Dukes and strong willed women occupy the background, where high-function status and family discourse intertwine within formalities (of administrative foresight, expression) observed. **24 Characters**

Richard III

An in palace drama with King Richard the 3rd, Queen Elizabeth, and Queen Margret. Onto a haunting reunion, as the state processes royal executions. **61+ Characters**

The Life and Death of King John
King John and Queen Elinor entertain the royal court, where a bastard has come to make his day. Strategic deployments of influence are exemplified, as the bastard plots about until alerts, alarm corruption has delivered trouble makers known.

24 Characters

Romeo and Juliet
Lovers emerge within a city gripped with two feuding houses apposed. As turmoil are caught in bitter heat, the lover's. Bliss and undying pledge becomes them, onto the eternal soul (of love and romance). **33 Characters**

Othello
A hopeful Othello calls upon the favor of allies based on proposed merits, which called upon allies and foes to him. In a mixed response, allies and foes campaign both against Othello, becoming a bitter, personal tangle over a mislead love adventure representing the future of either fates

25 Characters

Macbeth
A desperate Macbeth ventures towards witches to tell fortune, returning to a castle haunted by ghost/old-spirits. Macbeth's worries become frightful nightmares, along the despair of the household around him.   **39 Characters**

Mark Antony and Cleopatra

The relations or affections of Mark Anthony and Cleopatra, onto the strategic interactions between Mark Anthony and Octavius. The discourse moves to the Octavius house, revealing Octavia, and later then, Pompey in the background. Overall the focus retains upon Mark Anthony, Cleopatra, and Octavius.   **56+ Characters**

Coriolanus

Citizens riot during a famine, while the state administrative intervenes and otherwise discourses the seriousness of the matter and war. Lady's calm the general ambience, until the sword is mobilized to defend the gates, , while the plight of people is nevertheless heard convincing Roman elites the problem is being found/fought within.   **60 Characters**

Pericles Prince of Tyre

A thoughtful/reflective Pericles interposes his good will and well-meaning nature, which leads him to visit fishermen friends, and onto state function. Pericles is then confronted, required to (take a plunge) to marry, embedding him deeper into ocean stock of sea life among sailors experience and merchant owners, investing his interest as babe, securing his destiny as then, future king   **44 Characters**

Cymbeline

Cymbeline, friend or loyalist to the first Caesars, is summoned into battle. Meanwhile there are personal matters to attend to within the noble house.   **41 Characters**

The Winter's Tale
A gossipy tale of high office, administrative daily insight onto the tender meaning of things and people an how they unite unwittingly at the discourse of their respected hierarchies of partnership. Profoundness therein inspiring the recounts of clown and child, as examples perhaps of what state administration and or nobility's company keeps.

34+ Characters

The Tempest
After an earth shattering storm, a fairy dwelling world is found. There magic and graces are there in song, glory and praises.   **21 Characters**

The Two Gentlemen of Verona
Loving beginnings, yet far too. General virtues going upwards in hierarchies, with overall chivalrous wits.

Twelfth Night
An evening in the company of sound gatherings, seemingly a docile manner recount version of noble delights. In similarities of the pose, composing an environment of insight and oversight.

Henry the 8th
Across chamber and palace, Dukes and lords, until Queen Katharine's and King Henry VIII's present their graces, conversing the Cardinal then. The signs then, an Elizabeth is born.

Richard II
King Richard the 2nd readies the armed forces at the sound of alarm, while later Henry IV is near for discussion. King Richard the 2nd and his groom.

Henry V
King Henry the 5th, as found across his palace, until a readiness for war. King Henry the 5th and the French King, with armies both have at it.

Henry VI, Part 1
Funeral of King Henry the 5th, Henry VI makes his approach to France. Henry VI fashions as thy lord protector.

Henry VI, Part 2
King Henry the 6th, where the Cardinal is seen mocking protectors with praise, as all the rage. Queen Margaret at King Henry VI, until the end.

Henry VI, Part 3
King Henry VI is busy fighting a succession of battles, France and England as having at it, yet again.

King Henry the 5th
King Henry 5 fight his way toward France, they reach the peaceful and loving responses of a French King.

Henry IV, Part 1
King Henry the 4th, from Palace to Pub, onto the battle fields again. Until there is no rebellion.

Henry IV, Part 2
Henry IV, from Palace, Priest and then tavern, he nevertheless finds some peace, after reflection. King Henry IV, and then King Henry V as fashionable by the end.

Titus Andronicus
A story of Romans and Goths, where roman sways give way. And then to see about Goths and proving worthiness.

28 Characters

Julius Caesar

Near the Final days of the 1st Caesar, and the continuation everlasting as through Octavius.

Hamlet

Hamlet, and his father the King, the father yet a Ghost. Hamlet, not so eager to join.

King Lear

King Lear, from palace to castle, to fighting the French in the field. After battle King Lear is in bed, the Doctor discourses, what lays then now, will have an impact upon the end.

Timon of Athens

A story set in Greece, a place of poets and cultured, good graces. From Arts and daily expressive, to political and charmed.

www.ingramcontent.com/pod-product-compliance
Lightning Source LLC
Chambersburg PA
CBHW051430290426
44109CB00016B/1499